SURVIVING CYBERWAR

Richard Stiennon

GOVERNMENT INSTITUTES
An imprint of
THE SCARECROW PRESS, INC.
Lanham • Toronto • Plymouth, UK
2010

G Government
    Institutes

Published by Government Institutes
An imprint of The Scarecrow Press, Inc.
A wholly owned subsidary of The Rowman & Littlefield Publishing Group, Inc.
4501 Forbes Boulevard, Suite 200, Lanham, Maryland 20706
www.govinstpress.com

Estover Road, Plymouth PL6 7PY, United Kingdom

British Library Cataloguing in Publication Information Available

Library of Congress Cataloging-in-Publication Data

Stiennon, Richard, 1959–
  Surviving cyberwar / Richard Stiennon.
     p. cm.
  Includes bibliographical references and index.
  ISBN 978-1-60590-674-4 (cloth : alk. paper) — ISBN 978-1-60590-688-1 (pbk. :
alk. paper) — ISBN 978-1-60590-675-1 (electronic)
  1. Information warfare—United States. 2. Cyberterrorism—United States—
Prevention. 3. Cyberspace—Security measures. 4. Computer networks—
Security measures—United States. 5. Civil defense—United States. I. Title.
  U163.S73 2010
  355.3'43—dc22   2010008783

CONTENTS

ACKNOWLEDGMENTS

I could not have written *Surviving Cyberwar* without the support of a wide community of security experts, analysts, and editors. The members of the Cyber War Forum Initiative (CWFI) on Linkedin provided valuable insights and resources on government preparedness. Thanks to Randy Stone for making the trip to Leavenworth, Kansas, to pick up copies of Timothy L. Thomas's books on China's cyber thinking.

Ed Maguire and Ahto Parl connected the dots to make my trip to Estonia a success. Thanks to Kunnar Kukk and Aari Lemmik for arranging a meeting at the Estonian Ministry of Defense, and pointing me to valuable information resources. And thanks to Margus Vaino of Santa Monica Networks in Tallinn for being my guide and host.

Joe Ponepinto provided the necessary coaching as I tackled my first book, contributing a writer's perspective to the flow and continuity.

I once sat on a panel on entrepreneurship with Berry Fowler, the founder of Sylvan Learning Centers. When Barry was asked "what was the biggest contributor to your success?" he responded, "A loving and supportive spouse." I have had the opportunity to realize the truth in that statement thanks to my wife, Karen Ethier, who provided not only the encouragement but much of the heavy lifting in proof reading, editing, and indexing *Surviving Cyberwar*. Thank you Karen.

I could not have dedicated myself to many hours of research, travel, and writing without the financial support of Verisign and their iDefense team who sponsored the writing of this book.

INTRODUCTION

This is the story of the birth of a new era of human conflict. As of August 8, 2008, cyber conflict, in conjunction with physical attacks between opposing nations, has begun. The singular instance of Russian-sourced attacks against the small country of Georgia is just one brief episode in a history that is developing so rapidly it is a full-time job just keeping pace. The biggest challenge to writing a book about this developing global situation is deciding when to stop. By the time this book is published there will be at least a dozen new and interesting episodes of organized attacks on government websites in the United States, South Korea, Israel, and Iran, and on social networks like Twitter and Facebook; infiltration and theft of critical data from the defense organizations of the world; and disruption of critical infrastructure. The December 2009 Aurora incident involving Google and China in just one such event.

So let this book set the stage for an understanding of those future events. There will be no scary scenarios of cybergeddon or impending threats to civilization. No hand-wringing over the lack of preparedness or spending, although those situations are the norm. The use of networks and technical attacks against the resources connected to them is an evolution in the history of warfare. This book chronicles that evolution.

Computers have played an important role in intelligence gathering and analysis, encryption and cryptanalysis, the design of nuclear warheads, and simulations of all-out war. Since the official commercialization of the Internet only 15 years ago, networks have changed the face of communication, publishing, commerce, and human interaction. Vast knowledge is available to anyone who can access the Internet. Stock trading and banking transactions have moved to the Internet. Critical infrastructure such as oil and gas transport, electrical production and transmission, and emergency communications have become inexorably tied to the Internet. The pervasiveness of connections to the Internet has created a digitized world that is vulnerable to disruption, either accidental or malicious.

This book tracks that rise of exposure to new network threats. It borrows from the vocabulary and thinking of military strategists from history, as well as the output of Chinese academics and generals, U.S. think tanks, and security researchers, to shed light on cyber threats that have transformed from the actions of individuals, to crowds, to nations as the potential for combining network and computer attacks with war-fighting capabilities.

Drawing from the steps nations are taking to first defend themselves and then take offensive measures, this book defines a plan for cyber preparedness that can be executed by nations, businesses, and even individuals who are caught up in the turmoil as their own critical resources—e-mail, Skype, Twitter, blogs—become collateral damage.

My own journey to an understanding of the danger posed by Internet connectivity began in 1994. I remember being perplexed by one of the first customers of RustNet, the Internet Service Provider (ISP) I founded in Michigan, who wanted to purchase a firewall. "What are you worried about?" was the question I asked. Then, while working for Netrex, one of the first Managed Security Service Providers (MSSP), I met the pioneers of cyber defense, the founders of ISS (Tom Noonan, Chris Klaus) and Check Point Software (Gil Shwed, Marius Nacht, and Shlomo Kramer), and worked with their products to help auto manufacturers and the U.S. Army Tank Automotive Command protect their own networks. As a white-hat hacker for Coopers and Lybrand (later PricewaterhouseCoopers), I spent several years on the road assessing the security of some of the largest companies in the United States. From 2000 to 2004 I found myself in an influential position at the largest information technology (IT) research firm, Gartner, talking to thousands of IT departments about their security issues including best practices, policies, and, most important, the tools to enforce those security policies. I advised security vendors such as Symantec, Network Associates (now McAfee), Cisco, and Check Point Software on their product strategies. This period saw the formalization of security practices in most large enterprises. I left Gartner in 2004 to join one of the companies developing new tools to fight a new scourge, spyware. My evangelical role at Webroot Software provided me an opportunity to visit Europe and Asia and gain an understanding of their approach to security (often ahead of the United States) and their contrasting sales and distribution models for security products. As chief marketing officer at Fortinet, I continued that role of preaching the rise of cyber threats and the changes to IT organizations, practices, and tools that were needed to counter those threats.

This journey led me to recognize that a visionary could step back and predict the future by projecting current trends. The number of people using the Internet would continue to grow, bandwidth utilization would continue to explode, richer media would be available, and more commercial transactions would transition to the network. At the same time, threats would change from viruses, to worms, to spyware/adware, to denial of service attacks, to identity theft, and finally to political, fanatic, and military use.

I was not that visionary. Winn Scharwtau, Gregory Rattray, Richard Forno, and others had the vision of a future when nation-states would use the Internet to attack each other. These authors were reviled by the security community; they were considered Chicken Littles, modern day Nostradamuses. Fearful of attracting the same reprobation, I remained in the ranks of the naysayers. My position was, "Why even think about something that could happen in the realm of science fiction when your networks are being decimated by hackers and cyber criminals today?" My stump speech on cyber threats was: We will not experience information warfare until two adjacent networked countries engage in network attacks concurrent with tanks rolling across their borders. When that happened on August 8, 2008, in the small state of South Ossetia, it became time to rethink cyber threats in the light of this new era of cyberwar.

There is a lot of evidence that the use of network warfare and cyber espionage are part of modern war-fighting strategies at least within China and the United States. Attacks against Chechen separatists, Estonia, Lithuania, both sides of the Israel-Palestine conflict, India, and Pakistan are part of the rising tide of cyber conflict. And finally, the preparations being made for defending against cyber attack and the reorganization of military reporting structures makes moot any argument that cyberwar is a fiction. Cyberwar is a reality.

TITAN RAIN AND
SHAWN CARPENTER

This chapter introduces Shawn Carpenter, cyber warrior, as he discovers that all is not right at Sandia Labs in 2004. Cyber spies have infiltrated many of the United States' research labs, military branches, and agencies. Shawn Carpenter was the first to discover the extent of the hacking. He became a confidential informant for the FBI and lost his job because of his actions.

If you entrench yourself behind strong fortifications, you compel the enemy to seek a solution elsewhere.

—Carl von Clausewitz

The story of cyberwar cannot be told without recounting Shawn Carpenter's story. While history seems to wrap its tendrils around the military-politico thinking of the People's Republic of China in the 1990s, the rise of cybercrime and the pervasiveness of the Internet, revolutionary upheaval in former Soviet satellite states, and the evolution of malware, everything comes together at one point: Shawn Carpenter's investigation into Titan Rain. Any study of Chinese espionage, any report from analysts, any cyber legislation or reorganization of military commands have stemmed from the actions of Shawn Carpenter in 2004.

In the early evening of January 13, 2005, Shawn Carpenter was escorted to the gate of Sandia National Laboratories outside Albuquerque, New Mexico. The life he had struggled to pull together had come unraveled. The setting but still warm Albuquerque sun failed to ease the chill he felt as he left the extensive compound that was Sandia. Within the 10-foot fence and surveillance cameras and armed guards of the top nuclear research lab in the United States were the computer rooms and servers that he had fought to protect from intruders as an IT security administrator. Only months before, he had discovered that Chinese hackers had infiltrated Sandia, and indeed, other U.S. government agencies, military installations, and defense contractors, and were systematically stealing the most critical research information dealing with matters as far reaching as missile defense systems and the Mars Reconnaissance Orbiter. His efforts to track down the cyber spies that were so freely breaking through Sandia's minimal defenses had led him into trouble. Now he had been abandoned by his colleagues at Sandia and contacts in Army counterintelligence, mysteriously forgotten by his FBI handlers, and fired from his job. His badge and onetime password token had been taken from him. His security clearance had been revoked, making it close to impossible to work for the government ever again. What perturbed him the most was that his work, backtracking foreign agents who had attacked over the Internet, was left unfinished. Critical systems were being targeted; Shawn knew how to watch the attackers and warn the targets. Now he was silenced.

Shawn is a self-admitted geek. He will jokingly say he was the type of kid that the bullies liked to throw in the dumpster in the school parking lot. He has a sparkle in his eye that belies the trouble he has experienced. He will explode into infectious high-pitched laughter and delights in investigating and exploring the world around him. Before he was 10 he and a neighbor kid had moved beyond building rockets with Estes solid engines and begun to experiment with developing their own liquid-fueled engines in the field adjacent to his house. That phase ended the day there was an accident and they set the field ablaze. His first computer, like that of so many of today's computer experts, was a Tandy TRS-80.

Shawn is a meticulous journal keeper. He has piles of journals that he has written recording his life and activities since he was in fifth grade. This propensity to document everything served him well later on, as we will see.

Despite his fascination with technology Shawn entered the University of South Dakota as a music major: a trumpet player. His first year in college proved unproductive, and Shawn decided to go to Lincoln, Nebraska, where he was first exposed to information technology in the computer science program at the University of Nebraska, and working for Syntel where he worked with IBM 3090 JCL (Job Control Language) and DB2. He says he just loved working with computers.

It was 1990 when Shawn first read *The Cuckoo's Egg*, by Clifford Stoll. Many a security geek found Stoll's story of the discovery and eventual capture of a Russia-based hacker who had infiltrated the Lawrence Berkeley National Laboratory computer networks to be a turning point in their careers. This book introduced the world to the dangers of a global network, the Internet, that allowed criminals from anywhere to trespass on computer networks and systematically steal information that they could sell or use to cause damage. Stoll had been a system administrator at National Lab and used what now seem to be archaic techniques like tapping a network access point with a thermal printer to record login activity that led to confirmation of his suspicion that someone was gaining unauthorized access to the Lab's systems. Shawn was profoundly influenced by Stoll's story and admits that one of the most important moments of his life was a two-hour conversation with Stoll that occurred after Shawn's own Cuckoo's Egg adventure.

Shawn has fond memories of CS251 at the University of Nebraska. He, like so many Comp Sci majors over the years, engaged in a cat-and-mouse game with the university computer system administrators as he continuously hacked their systems to plant bugs and steal login credentials from other students. You can hear the story from just about any computer geek. They program the mainframe to display a fake login screen and leave the terminal running. An unsuspecting first-year student sits down at the terminal and logs in with their username and password, which are recorded in a file for later access. The student accounts provide limited "funny-money" that the students spend for computing cycles to complete their assignments. By transferring those funds to their own accounts, the hackers can have even more fun with the university computers.

It was another year before Shawn was pulled from Nebraska to Albuquerque by a cousin who said he had a job for him at Honeywell

Defense Avionics, a defense contractor. But the job was no longer available when he got to Albuquerque. In urgent need of a job he turned to the want ads.

One ad caught his eye and he quickly dialed the 800 number supplied. When he discovered that he had called a recruiter for the Armed Forces he quickly hung up. That was not for him. But then he spent an introspective hour going over his options. Maybe what he needed was the discipline of the military. Maybe he "needed someone to put a boot in his ass." He called back.

On June 12, 1991, Shawn Carpenter enlisted in the U.S. Navy and reported to boot camp in Orlando, Florida. He spent six years serving on nuclear-powered surface ships as a nuclear engineer. His job was engine maintenance on nuclear power piles and steam turbines. The technical demands proved no problem for a born tinkerer. Dosage meters, handling radioactive components in protective gear, and working on the most sophisticated engines in the world was no problem for someone with a curious mind and a taste for technology.

When the term of service ended in 1997 he followed up on e-mail contacts with former shipmates working at Sandia and landed a job as a contractor for Sandia. He was a radiological technician, a job that leveraged his experience with radioactive environments. That is when he met his soon-to-be wife, Jennifer Jacobs, a PhD in nuclear engineering and an Army Reserve officer.

In 1998 research and academic institutions everywhere began to experience technological brain drain as Silicon Valley experienced a "dot com boom" and sucked computer savvy geeks into its engine of innovation and wealth creation. Sandia had a policy of hiring from within and opened up an opportunity to join the IT security staff that Shawn jumped at. He was the top-ranked graduate of their retraining program and became a full time "Sandian" as he left the ranks of contractors.

Shawn became responsible for day-to-day administration of Sandia's Intrusion Detection Systems (IDS). He was fulfilling the role that Clifford Stoll played at Berkeley but with much more mature tools including the open-source SNORT and commercial tools from Internet Security Systems (ISS, now a part of IBM).

IDS systems monitor computer networks and servers. They have a long list of signatures of possible attacks and create an alert every time network traffic or server activity matches one of those signatures. A signature is nothing more than a string of characters that an analyst has determined are unique to a particular attack. One frustrating aspect of IDS systems is that they alert after the attack is underway. They do nothing to block or prevent an attack. It is up to the IDS analyst to track down the meaning of every alert.

In the summer of 2003, Shawn was assigned to a special task force that investigated some intrusions into Sandia's parent corporation, Lockheed Martin. He deployed to a Lockheed facility in Florida to assist in analyzing the attacks and closing down the holes that the attackers had found. Shawn discovered that some of the attacks originated in China. On that machine he found the results of a network scan of the internal network of the U.S. Army Base, Fort Dix, contained in a file labeled 1.txt. When he returned from that assignment after successfully identifying the attacks and hardening Lockheed's systems against further incursions he recognized that Sandia was also under attack from some of the same sources as identified by their IP addresses.

It did not take long for Shawn Carpenter to detect in his IDS logs that there was something seriously amiss at Sandia Labs. Someone was launching very sophisticated attacks against networks and servers within his purview and stealing data. He investigated those attacks and found they were coming from a computer server in South Korea. Knowing from his previous research at Lockheed about some of the tools the hackers used, Shawn was able to access the hacking tools loaded on the South Korean machine and from there see the files stored on the machine. There were files from hundreds of U.S. military, research, and commercial networks including Fort Dix, the Redstone Arsenal, the Defense Contract Management Agency, and the World Bank.

If you discover military espionage activities on your networks, whom do you call? Do you talk to your boss? The director of Sandia Labs? Shawn went to his immediate supervisor who told him, "We don't care about national security, we only care about Sandia."

The world of spies, military intelligence, and cyber warfare is a dark one. You do not know who is watching or whom to trust. U.S. National Research Labs had been experiencing embarrassing spy-related incidents. Just four years earlier Lockheed Martin, Sandia's parent corporation, had paid fines of $13 million for violating export restrictions on satellite technology to China. Perhaps that led to the reluctance on the part of Sandia to share information with other U.S. networks about possible incursions they had experienced.

That evening Shawn talked it over with his wife. Was ignoring the information he had obtained the right thing to do? They decided it was not.

Shawn had to call someone he trusted. That someone was a friend he had worked with who was a contractor providing counterespionage services for the military. With that step, Shawn became involved in the veiled, spy vs. spy world of military counterintelligence and eventually the FBI.

Shawn's intelligence about Chinese spying was of immediate interest to the military. They started to communicate with him and share tradecraft that would allow them to benefit from his knowledge and ability to gather more information. With encouragement from the U.S. military, Shawn turned his home computer lab into a counterespionage launching pad. He worked on his own time responding to requests from the military, sometimes getting calls in the early morning asking him to investigate a suspect IP address.

Despite the mystery and technical jargon that surrounds computer hacking, it is easy for anyone to learn the tools of the trade. That is one of the frightening things about computer weaknesses: they are remarkably easy to exploit. Alex Kahn, CEO and founder of Palantir Technologies, a company that develops software tools for tracking research and forensic investigation, says, "The Internet has democratized espionage." See the accompanying "anatomy of a hack," "the new anatomy of a hack," and "the new, new anatomy of a hack" to understand the cookbook approach that most hackers use to break into systems.

Already well versed in these techniques, and with in-depth knowledge of networking protocols, Shawn proceeded to track the hackers who were attacking Sandia, the World Bank, the Army Research Lab, and the other networks. From IDS logs he could see the IP addresses of machines used to scan Sandia resources. He would scan those machines, look for vulnerabilities and discover hacking tool kits already installed on them. He would then crack the passwords for those tool kits and use them to gain access to the compromised machines the hackers were using to launch attacks. Once in, he could monitor the activity of the hackers who had installed them! He could see the source

There are three different attack scenarios: Outside network-based attack, outside Trojan Horse, and the insider attack. Shawn's adversaries used variations of all these.

Anatomy of an Attack

The network-based attack has four phases. The first is a footprint analysis. The attacker learns as much about the target as he or she can. In the case of Sandia Labs this could be a long process. Sandia supports IT infrastructure for 10,000 employees and contractors. Information about Sandia can be found at their website, on Wikipedia, the Congressional Record, and numerous documents maintained by government contractors. IP address ranges, domains, and technology used can be discerned from online resources. Several incidents over the years have involved Chinese spies who worked on-site. A spy on the premises could provide valuable information about locations of critical designs and data. The purpose of a footprint analysis is to enumerate the target network and identify key gateways and servers to be attacked.

The next phase is scanning. Open source tools such as Nessus, Metasploit, even whois clients, nslookup, and nMap are used to scan IP address ranges to find responsive hosts, and then scan each port on each host to determine the version number of the operating system (OS), and common applications that are listening and responding. From there, known vulnerabilities in these systems are exploited using freely available tools or specifically engineered attacks. A rootkit is usually installed that allows the attacker to control the resource remotely as if they were the system owner.

The final phase in the network-based attack is to cull information and retrieve it. A wily hacker will cover his or her tracks by changing logs that could have recorded their activity and erasing all traces of the tools they used.

As shown, the network-based attack can be labor intensive and requires the use of fairly sophisticated tools. A new methodology has arisen that is even easier to execute.

The New Anatomy of an Attack

The custom Trojan has become the most powerful tool in this new methodology. See chapter 4 on the Israeli Trojan affair, UK industrial scale attacks, and GhostNet, the Chinese-run network of 1,200 compromised hosts in dozens of countries. This attack also begins with the footprint analysis or reconnaissance phase. The next phase is to induce an insider to load a customized Trojan Horse onto their computer. This can be accomplished in many ways.

1. *Drive-by download.* E-mail spam messages are sent to the target with links to interesting sites. The destination of those links are compromised machines that harbor code that exploits a vulnerability in the user's browser or Adobe Acrobat, java, or media player software. The code installs a custom Trojan Horse.

(continued)

2. *Two-phase attack.* A custom virus is e-mailed to recipients within the target organization. It spreads through e-mail servers and infects internal e-mail accounts, harvesting internal e-mail addresses from address books. The second phase is a crafty e-mail that appears to be legitimately from someone in the organization. Attached to this second e-mail is the custom Trojan.
3. *Social engineering.* This is the method used in the Israeli Trojan affair, using Michael Haephrati's code. The attacker communicates either by e-mail or phone with the targeted insider and forewarns him or her that an e-mail is on its way with an important document attached. The recipient opens the attachment and infects their machine with the custom Trojan.
4. *Candy drop.* This clever technique uses a USB thumb drive to deliver the payload. The thumb drive could be dropped in a parking lot, left at a local bar, or sent directly to the targeted insider. Once plugged in to the insider's computer it automatically installs the custom Trojan. This technique was used successfully against the U.S. Central Command and infected military operations around the world.

It is very important to understand the devastating power of custom Trojan Horses. Most organizations have invested much of their security budget in anti-virus (AV) systems that identify versions of the hundreds of thousands of viruses, worms, and Trojans that have been discovered in the last two decades. All an attacker has to do is modify their malware until it no longer contains a known signature (just a string of characters unique to each piece of known malware). Standard AV software will not detect malware customized in this way.

Once installed, the custom Trojan Horse downloads additional software that can record keystrokes, screen shots, and even voice and video from the infected machine. Files can be searched and key information sent back to the attacker.

The New, New Anatomy of an Attack

One final methodology used by attackers is the special case of the insider attack. In this case the attacker is already a trusted member of the organization. This could be a spy in the pay of an opponent, cleaning staff, or a contractor or visitor. They use their privileges and network access to scan, identify, and exploit repositories of critical information. An insider can upload keystroke logging software on fellow employees' machines or even install small hardware keystroke loggers in the USB ports or where a keyboard attaches to the back of a desktop machine. The risks of discovery and prosecution are higher than in remote attacks, but the chances of success are much higher for an inside agent. Insiders have successfully stolen secret information, credit card data, and even altered systems to allow them to execute unauthorized trades as in the case of Jérôme Kerviel of Société Générale. A Goldman Sachs employee, Sergey Aleynikov, is accused of stealing secret stock-trading algorithms using his position as a trusted insider.

IP address the hackers were coming from and could then concentrate on the next link up a chain that took him all the way to South Korea, Italy, Taiwan, and China.

Shawn was motivated by a sense of urgency. Exfiltrated files do not reside long on servers. By reacting quickly, without waiting for permission, he was pursuing intruders to the best of his ability. And of course, there is the example set by Clifford Stoll, a much-admired hero who independently tracked down the hacker who had broken into Livermore Berkeley Labs.

But Shawn was not working independently. He was fully aware of the seriousness of what he was doing and the national security implications of Chinese hackers' infiltrating the nuclear weapons research labs of the United States. What happened to Shawn Carpenter as he pursued foreign cyber attackers is very revealing about the state of the United States' cyber preparedness—or lack thereof. Shawn Carpenter was first encouraged by the military and then the FBI to pursue his adversaries and then abandoned by them to face repercussions that led to his expulsion from Sandia and losing his security clearances.

On that day when Shawn decided to investigate the cyber espionage activities targeting Sandia he realized that he could not work alone. He contacted a friend who was employed as a contractor in the U.S. Army Research Labs Center for Intrusion Monitoring and Protection. He was quickly pulled into their operations and given instructions as to how to proceed. He set up shop in his house outside of Albuquerque and began his meticulously documented cyber activities.

His contact within the military introduced Shawn to the FBI, and a meeting was set up at the FBI field office in Albuquerque in October, 2004. Many of the targets Shawn had identified were already under investigation by the FBI. It turns out that Shawn had stepped into the middle of Titan Rain, an extensive cyber espionage effort already detected, as we will see, by many governments around the world. But Shawn had gone further than they had by infiltrating the attacking servers. Over the next three months Shawn worked with the FBI, which pumped him for information that supported their investigations. Shawn was a confidential informant (CI).

Shawn met regularly with his FBI handlers in various public locations around Albuquerque: restaurants, hotel rooms, coffee shops, and the basement of the Law Library of the University of New Mexico. But the coming and going by separate exits and the quick breakup of meetings if they saw someone they knew proved too disruptive, and the meetings were moved to Shawn and Jennifer's home.

In November of 2004 the FBI notified Sandia that they were working with Shawn on these cyber investigations. Initially Sandia counterintelligence people were inclined to be supportive, but when they informed Sandia management of what was going on things quickly came to a head. By January 13, 2005, Shawn Carpenter was terminated from his employment with Sandia National Laboratories for insubordination and performing illegal acts; charges that were never supported and ultimately were rescinded after a lengthy lawsuit and jury trial that completely vindicated Shawn.

Unfortunately, Sandia's reaction to learning about Shawn's participation in FBI investigations led to cessation of all of Shawn's work to track down and understand the activities of foreign agents who had successfully hacked into the Army Research Labs, Lockheed Martin, NASA, the World Bank, and other networks. Perhaps subsequent attacks on the Pentagon, the Joint Strike Fighter project, and Army Command in various theaters around the world could have been avoided or at least contained quickly if Sandia, military counterintelligence, and the FBI had worked together. The military, which had initially created the label Titan Rain, changed the name and slapped a classified designation on it so now even the name of the work instigated by Shawn Carpenter is secret.

As cyber warfare thinking, techniques, and actions unfold throughout the world, Titan Rain will be remembered as the early warning that went unheeded. Action taken in 2005 to step up U.S. cyber countermeasures could have led to a much stronger position and more knowledgeable approach to the Comprehensive Cyber Security Initiative announced in 2007 by the Bush administration.

Titan Rain was just a glimpse into the widespread cyber espionage and development of cyber attack capability witnessed throughout the world.

THE RED WARS

China has a long history of military research and academic pursuit of the Revolution in Military Affairs. In this chapter, we explore that thinking, the events of 2001, the ensuing rise of cyber espionage, and China's complicity in this new era of cyber hostilities.

> U.S. military and government networks and computer systems continue to be the target of intrusions that appear to have originated from within the PRC.
>
> —Admiral Robert F. Willard, U.S. Navy

We leave Shawn Carpenter, cyber warrior, abandoned by his country and fighting to exonerate his name and reputation, to explore the beginnings of Chinese cyber threats to the United States.

On April 1, 2001, a U.S. E3 reconnaissance plane was patrolling over the coast of mainland China. Its mission: to intercept and harvest Chinese military, commercial, and government communications traffic for later analysis by the legions of intelligence workers in the U.S. National Security Agency (NSA) tasked with modern spying missions. While the CIA is supposed to be infiltrating foreign organizations and promoting U.S. interests on the ground, and the FBI is tasked with fighting organized crime, child pornographers, and terrorists on U.S. soil, the NSA was created to intercept hostile communications, decode them if necessary, and evaluate them for evidence of threats to the United States. That is a big task and, as anyone who has attempted to drive past the Patuxent exit on Highway 295 to the NSA's headquarters in Langley, Virginia, during commuting hours knows, it involves many people.

While on routine patrol over the South China Sea the U.S. Navy E3 was intercepted by a Chinese F8 fighter jet. The pilot, Wu Nos, guided his multibillion-Yuan jet into a collision course with the unarmed E3 and knocked it out of the sky. The fighter pilot died. No one was injured in the EP-3E, but it was forced to make an emergency landing on China's Hainan Island. The ensuing diplomatic clash was reminiscent of the intrigue and accusations that occurred in 1960, when Captain Gary Powers, flying the top secret U-2 spy plane, was shot down by a Soviet air-to-air missile.[1]

This time there was no secrecy. The United States demanded a return of its airplane and its crew. The Chinese demanded a U.S. apology. What happened next is still murky because the United States was not, and is not, equipped to monitor, detect, or respond to cyber attacks in a comprehensive or coordinated manner. To understand the situation we must cast back in time to the state of Internet security circa 2001.

The Internet was still fresh in 2001. The tech bubble, catalyzed by the Internet, was just bursting as sock puppets and home delivery grocery stores became symbols for the dot bomb. Yet there was no cybercrime, only hints of the coming onslaught of adware and spyware, and technologies like patch management were in their infancy.

Patch management—what a crazy idea! Every time there was a new vulnerability announced in a major platform like Solaris (Sun Microsystems) or Windows (Microsoft), security experts would berate the industry for not updating all of their servers and desktop computers immediately. But that was a difficult task. Microsoft, the real culprit in the vulnerability problem, would release security updates to its multitudinous server and desktop products almost every week. Updating a server meant taking it off-line, usually on weekends, installing the patch, testing it, and putting it back online. Every time a server was taken off-line and reconfigured administrators ran the risk of damaging something either on the server or in the myriad of computers and networks that relied on that server. Some organizations had thousands of servers, and no means of quickly and efficiently upgrading them. And most administrators believed that they were neither targets of hackers nor had any information of value to cyber spies.

That argument of not being a target for attackers is an oft-repeated refrain that is heard at each step of the escalation in cyber threats. Time and events are tearing away at that belief in the security of invisibility and obscurity. One lesson this book hopes to teach is that cyberwar is something that affects every organization. Preparing for it and making investments to counter the types of targeted attacks described here is just the next level in the cat-and-mouse game known as IT security. What happened on May 1, 2001, was the beginning of the erosion in "security by obscurity" as a means of avoiding investment in security.

At the heart of the ensuing Chinese cyber attacks were well-publicized flaws in the way Microsoft had implemented its Internet Information Server, or IIS. IIS was Microsoft's web server software used by tens of thousands of organizations to publish web pages using HTML, the language of websites. In retrospect it seems quaint and evocative of an innocence no longer present in today's world that security industry analysts such as John Pescatore of Gartner could talk about timelines that played out over months. The first stage of the threat would be the discovery of a vulnerability. Then it would be published, either by the vendor of the vulnerable system, usually coincident with a patch, or by the hacker/researcher who discovered it, after which there would be the discovery of exploit code or a methodology by some nefarious group or hacker "in the wild." The final stage would be the use of the exploit, either to spread a worm or virus or in direct attacks. Today, of course, all of those stages have been compressed into hours or even occur in reverse: exploit used, discovered, and finally a patch published.

By May 1, 2001, the vulnerability in Microsoft IIS had been published, patches had been issued by Microsoft, and exploits developed by various researchers. The tools to attack any Windows-based web server were well known and easy to obtain and use. And, because of the lack of previous experience with attacks and the enormous hassle and expense associated with patching thousands of servers, almost all Windows web servers were still vulnerable. What ensued was the first outbreak of cyber hostilities between China and the United States.

The press at the time treated the first cyber skirmish as an extension of the hacking-for-fun that they had been reporting on for years, as teenage boys defaced websites in a cyber age equivalent of spray painting graffiti on buildings, subway cars, and overpasses: all in good fun with the damage limited to embarrassment for the hapless targets. But this was different, even in its reported guise of innocent tit-for-tat as U.S.-based hackers and Chinese sources of attacks engaged in widespread defacements of each other's public websites. The motivation was outrage over the E3 spy plane incident. According to Xu Wu,

> On 26 April, H.U.C. Honker Union of China] announced on its site that Chinese hackers would wage a seven-day self-defense war against American websites. The major targets included hundreds of American government and military websites. The attacking time was set at 9:00 PM on 30 April, when a seven-day Labor Day holiday started in China.[2]

Neither the timing of these attacks, coincident with the International Socialist Movement's celebration of May Day, nor the scope of the attacks against U.S. targets can be ignored. Hundreds of vulnerable U.S. agencies, branches of the military, and commercial entities that had chosen domain names that identified them as "American" succumbed to defacement at the hands of China-based hackers. While today the evidence remains circumstantial, in retrospect the hacker war of 2001 bears all the signs of being coordinated by (or at least encouraged by) the Chinese government with two purposes: to probe the cyber defenses of the United States and determine just what could be gleaned from its vulnerable servers and networks, and to gauge the response of the U.S. government—diplomatic, military, or economic—to an incursion on its soil. The May 1 cyber skirmish must have proved a gold mine for China's equivalent of the NSA. The U.S. response? Nothing. No diplomats recalled, no warnings, no talk of invasion of territory, and most tellingly, no military repercussions. None.

Sites that were attacked include California Independent System Operator (Cal-ISO), the state manager of long-distance electricity transmission; the Department of Labor; Department of Health and Human Services; and the website of the U.S. Surgeon General. As noted above, these sites were targets of the Chinese "Honker Union," which had called for attacks a week earlier and had posted three pages of U.S. targets on their website.

Soon after these direct attacks, a worm was released on the Internet that also attacked IIS-based web servers. It contained references to China, as did the Nimda worm of November 2009.

Let us enter the realm of supposition here. Suppose that China has long-term plans, strategies, and, especially, motivation to expand its frontiers and global influence. Suppose that China is concerned by the superpower status of the United States and in some way is threatened by the power of democracy as a belief system as well as the individual states that practice it. Suppose that China viewed itself then and now as a country that must advance its technology—military, scientific, and commercial—to compete on a global scale. Would not China engage in industrial espionage to leapfrog its global competitors? Taiwan, France, Germany, Britain, Australia, New Zealand, and India would all come under attack from Chinese cyber forces if any of this were the case. And, indeed, all of these countries have reported loss of servers and critical data to cyber attacks emanating from China.

The United States maintains a widespread community of China analysts in its intelligence agencies, academic institutions, defense contractors, and freelance contributors to "open source" research. They pour over manuscripts and documents published in Chinese and English to enhance the understanding of the last great communist regime. To repurpose Winston Churchill's famous characterization of the Soviet Union: China is a "riddle wrapped in a mystery inside an enigma."

Since 2001, these China analysts have devoted their efforts to understanding China's thinking on modern warfare and, in particular, information warfare. The body of knowledge they have to work with is extensive and surprising in the level of logic and careful consideration that China's military theoreticians have applied to what they call the Revolution in Military Affairs (RMA).

Let's go back a couple of thousand years and examine Sun Tzu's original treatise, *The Art of War*. In his book *The Craft of Intelligence*, Allen W. Dulles, father of the CIA, writes:

> To Sun Tsu belongs the credit not only for the first remarkable analysis of the ways of espionage but also for the first written recommendations regarding an organized intelligence service. He points out that the master of intelligence will employ all five kinds of agents simultaneously; he calls this the "Divine Skein." The analogy is to a fishnet consisting of many strands all joined to a single cord. He comments on counter-intelligence, on psychological warfare, on deception, on security, on fabricators, in short, on the whole craft of intelligence.[3]

Indeed, Sun Tzu devoted a separate section of *The Art of War* to the employment of spies. Dulles then says: "It is no wonder that Sun Tzu's book is a favorite of Mao-Tse-tung and is required reading for Chinese

Communist tacticians. In their conduct of military campaigns and of intelligence collection, they clearly put into practice the teachings of Sun Tzu," this from the man in charge of the United States' intelligence operations during the Cold War, when China and the USSR were his primary adversaries.

In his 2004 paper "Sun Tzu's Strategic Thought and Its Inspiration for Informationized Warfare," presented at the "Sixth International Seminar on Sun Tzu's Art of War," Chai Yuqui of the Nanjiing Army Command Academy called Sun Tzu a grand strategist without parallel in history.[4]

Chinese theoreticians have been considering the implications of information warfare for two decades. Look at the titles of some of their research:

Wang Qingsong, *Modern Military-Use High Technology*, 1993
Zhu Youwen, Feng Yi, and Xu Dechi, *Information War under High Tech Conditions*, 1994
Li Qingshan, *New Military Revolution and High Tech War*, 1995
Wang Pufeng, *Information Warfare and the Revolution in Military Affairs*, 1995
Zhu Xiaoli and Zhao Xiaozhuo, *The United States and Russia in the New Military Revolution*, 1996
Dai Shenglong and Shen Fuzhen, *Information Warfare and Information Security Strategy*, 1996
Shen Weiguang, *On New War*, 1997

According to China researcher Timothy L. Thomas, Dr. Shen Weiguang is known in China as the father of information warfare (IW) theory. In 1995, Shen wrote an introductory article on IW for the People's Liberation Army (PLA) daily newspaper. In it, Shen states that the main target of IW is the enemy's cognitive and trust systems and the goal is to exert control over his actions.

Thomas discovered more interesting thinking in a 2004 article by General Xu Xiaoyan, the former head of the Communications Department of the Chinese General Staff. Xu dissects the realm of information warfare. At the granular level he points out the need for:

Network confrontation technology—intercepting, utilizing, corrupting, and damaging the enemy's information and using false information, viruses, and other means to sabotage normal information system functions through computer networks.[5]

Thomas goes on to offer the following observations:

> If Xu's suggestions were accepted, then one might expect to see more active reconnaissance and intelligence activities on the part of the PLA (as seems to be occurring!)

That exclamation point is Thomas's.

THE SIMPLEST, MOST EFFECTIVE ESPIONAGE TOOL

We now turn to a curious set of events that occurred on Memorial Day weekend in 2005: the Haephrati Trojan fiasco in Israel.

An Israeli author, Amnon Jackont, noticed that some of his unpublished works were circulating on the Internet and called the police because he suspected his ex-stepson-in-law, Michael Haephrati, was responsible. The police failed to find the spyware on Jackont's PC that was uploading files, e-mail, and keystroke logs to a server in the UK. But Jackont's stepdaughter's (Haephrati's ex-wife) PC eventually yielded to investigation, as it was infected as well. The police tracked the transmissions from the Trojan horse residing on her computer back to FTP (File Transfer Protocol) servers in the UK and Germany, which they discovered contained files from many Israeli companies that indicated they were infected with spyware as well. The Israeli police investigated further and found that computers in those companies were infected with Haephrati's Trojan. They arrested the heads of three private investigator firms and charged them with installing spyware within target organizations. That led to the arrests and questioning of executives at the firms that had hired the private investigators.

Here is how the Haephrati Trojan horse was being used by the private investigators. They would contract with Haephrati, who would then generate a "custom" piece of software that was undetectable by commercial anti-virus programs. They would take the executable file and send it to target recipients after calling them and warning them that they were sending over a file. This is one of the most audacious uses of "social engineering" techniques ever. (Social engineering is the use of nontechnical subterfuge to get people to reveal information or allow access to their systems.) Targets of these attacks included cell phone, satellite television, and bottled water companies. The recipients of the e-mails would open the attachment and immediately become infected with the Haephrati Trojan software that would proceed to upload files and record keystroke logs to the servers hosted by Michael Haephrati for later viewing and download by the private investigators and, presumably, transfer to their clients.

This incident is important because it provides insight into how effective custom software can be for espionage. Note that there is no need to exploit a vulnerability in the target's computer. All that is required is for the recipient to be induced to install the software. We will return to this methodology when we discuss the GhostNet research report on the infiltration of the Dalai Lama's office by Chinese operatives in chapter 4.

The uncovering of the Haephrati Trojan fiasco was followed almost immediately by an announcement by the National Infrastructure Security Co-ordination Centre (NISCC) in the UK that a similar attack methodology had been in operation for at least two years, targeting UK businesses and government agencies. The attacks came in two waves. The first was a custom virus designed to spread within the target organization, harvest e-mail addresses from address books, and forward them back to home base in "The Far East." Once again it is critical to note that despite the widespread deployment of anti-virus solutions, most of these are signature based and therefore unable to protect an organization against a targeted attack using customized malware. The second wave was the social engineering step. E-mails would be sent with spoofed "from" addresses as if they were sent from someone internal to the target organization. Their payload would be the Trojan horse meant to steal documents, record keystrokes, and hand over control to a remote operator. While NISCC was reticent to point fingers at the largest country in Asia, it is now evident that China was the culprit in these attacks. China had been engaged in industrial-scale cyber espionage since at least 2003. Shawn Carpenter's discovery of incidents that were one small part of the Titan Rain was the tip of the iceberg.

As we shall see in later chapters, China is not picky about its targets. In conjunction with one of the fastest rises of any economy since Japan after World War II, China has been systematically invading and stealing from the computer resources of the entire industrialized world.

Most of that world is woefully unprepared for defending against this type of espionage. In the next chapter we explore three simple security maxims and their application in defending against cyber espionage.

COUNTERING CYBER ESPIONAGE

In this chapter we discuss the use of computers and networks for illicit information gathering. The techniques and tools of cyber espionage are introduced. We enumerate countermeasures to cyber espionage that all organizations can deploy.

> *For decades to come the spy world will continue to be the collective couch where the subconscious of each nation is confessed.*
>
> —John Le Carré

Cyber espionage, the use of computers and networks to steal information, is not limited to nation-states that are in conflict. Business competitors, stock speculators, sports franchises, and employees may be motivated to spy on each other. This is the first of three chapters that delve into the active measures your business, your government agency, and even individuals can take to avoid losing data to cyber spies. As we will see in chapter 14, "Cyber Preparedness," government agencies have neglected their security and left themselves wide open to cyber espionage.

Cyber espionage predates the Internet. Using computers, data storage media, and networks to steal information is the broadest definition of cyber espionage. A slight nuance separates the idea of cyber espionage from an important other type of data theft: cybercrime. Stealing credit card information, identities, and bank account credentials is different from cyber espionage. While the defenses against cybercrime may coincide with espionage defenses, the motivation and types of data stolen are different. Countering cyber espionage requires a much more comprehensive approach to data security.

The target for espionage is information that has value to the attacker. It could be military intelligence such as troop movements, missile deployments, logistics, or force strength. It could be diplomatic data such as treaty intentions. It could be industrial-military information such as missile or ship designs. It could be commercial information like sales figures, customer lists, secret formulae, processes, or suppliers. Internally it could be salary information, union bargaining positions, or performance reviews. The spying entity seeks to gain an advantage by exploiting knowledge gained through surreptitious use of computers and networks. Cyber espionage is just one element of intelligence gathering, which includes aerial reconnaissance, radio and TV monitoring, infiltration, diplomatic exchange, and cloak-and-dagger activities.

The lines can be blurred between cyber and physical spying when, for instance, a foreign agent infiltrates an organization and uses modern tools to record and transmit stolen information. When senior level FBI agent Robert Hanssen was finally apprehended for spying, we learned that he used his Palm III device to store information and used encrypted floppy disks to transfer secrets to his Soviet controllers.

Allen Dulles said, "the essence of espionage is access," and indeed that translates into today's terms when access to information has grown at extraordinary rates and the task of restricting access to critical information has grown at the same rate.

A HYPOTHETICAL SPY OPERATION

Let's build a use case for the sly agent whose purpose is to steal an organization's data. The target could be a government research lab such as Sandia, it could be the office of a religious leader (the Dalai Lama), it could be an automotive manufacturer, or the Defense Department. Let's name our cyber spy Izzy Espy. Izzy works for a foreign government. He works from home but has limited access to the Internet so he spends a lot of time in Internet cafés. His mission is very loosely defined. He has been asked to gather information from anywhere he can within the United States. He is not to worry about the value of the information. He is just to spend his time uncovering vulnerabilities, exploiting them, and seeing where his activity takes him. The data analysis is carried out within the halls of a military intelligence agency, which determines what to do with the data once it has been thoroughly analyzed. Industrial processes and plans are forwarded to local manufacturers. Missile plans and fleet deployment data are added to the body of military intelligence being built up. Political intelligence is forwarded to Foreign Affairs. Mr. Espy is paid a monthly salary that is just enough to support him and purchase the equipment he needs. He might dabble in a little credit card and bank theft on the side. He does not necessarily know whom he is working for, but he can guess.

As a first step, Mr. Espy works from a list of targets. He browses their websites and starts to probe their outward-facing servers. Usually this quickly leads to results. A vulnerability in a Web server gives him access to a backend database, and he starts stealing customer data. But he needs more, so he starts very quietly to scan the target's network from outside. He is looking for IP addresses, machines that are answering on open ports, and vulnerabilities in those services that are accessible from the Internet. When he finds a router, mail server, or application server that is vulnerable, he gains access and escalates his privileges until he has the same access as an internal system administrator. He steals any data that resides on that machine and proceeds to install scanning software that will let him find additional targets on the inside of the network. From there he gains control of individual desktop machines owned by key personnel. It could be military communications, wire transfer personnel at a bank, or the CEO's laptop. He installs spy programs that record everything typed on the keyboard, steals files, and even turns on the laptop's microphone and camera. He proceeds to grab usernames and passwords from those users. Over a short period of several days he has obtained access to an organization's IT infrastructure equivalent to that held by the most trusted insider. All of that organization's documents, designs, plans, financials, trading algorithms, processes, and data end up in the hands of an intelligence operation overseas.

Mr. Espy used the Internet to gain access to an organization's networks. He attacked vulnerable servers and desktops, and he used stolen user credentials to gain access to critical data. How is an organization to counter espionage of this ilk?

Because protecting data from being acquired by an enemy is an all-encompassing task, it is important to begin with a simple set of security maxims that can guide technology investments, process implementation, and enforcement measures. There are three such principles. They serve to simplify the task of designing a response to a threat. The principles are derived from the concept of decoupling, an engineering term that describes the simplification of a large problem by breaking it down into its component parts. By decoupling we can tackle the security problem one step at a time.

First Principle of Simple Security: Good Network Security Assumes That Endpoints Are Hostile

A secure network in its ideal form would be one that carried no traffic that included worms, viruses, port scans, or hack attacks. While an ideal, it is the model that should be strived for. The best technology available today applies a series of filters and triggers to prevent bad traffic from entering a network either from the outside or from an endpoint attached to the inside. The technologies reside in multiple products or a single unified threat management system that applies multiple filters all at once. The typical business has already deployed the following at their access point to the Internet and other networks:

Firewall

A firewall, in its simplest form, contains a set of security policies that define acceptable source IP addresses, destination IP addresses, and port numbers. The list of source IP addresses could be for trusted service providers such as a bank or trading partner. The destination IP addresses could be that of the mail server, the Web server, or some other device. When the protocols of the Internet, TCP/IP, were first devised it was thought that every new application people could invent would use a separate identifier called a port number, selected from a possible 65,536 choices. Low level ports below 1023 were set aside for specific applications. Thus, port 25 is reserved for e-mail and port 80 for Web browsing. Firewalls are supposed to have a set of explicitly allowed rules and everything else should be blocked. In security speak this is the "Deny All That Is Not Explicitly Allowed" rule.

URL Content Filtering

The original purpose of blocking access to particular Web addresses (URLs) was to prevent unproductive employee activities associated with "surfing the Web." Filters were created with categories of sites such as sports, pornography, hate, news, or shopping–giving the organization control over what types of activities end users could engage in. Over recent years these filters acquired a security purpose as well in that they could prevent people from browsing to known malicious sites that could completely bypass the firewall and install viruses and Trojans via the user's Web browser. Further enhancements to URL content filtering devices not only block access to known malicious sites, but detect and remove malware from being downloaded from any site.

Anti-Malware

E-mail, instant messages, and many other services can be used to transmit viruses, worms, and Trojans. Inline network devices are usually employed to prevent malware from getting past the gateway.

Anti-Spam

Both spam and malware are often caught and scrubbed at the mail server, but network devices can be deployed to filter out spam as well.

Intrusion Prevention

Network-based attacks involve using a crafty exploit to compromise a system within the organization. The attack could be executed manually or it could be from a worm or service. An Intrusion Prevention System (IPS) identifies and filters out these attacks.

Even after all of these filters are applied with one or many devices there are still possible vectors of attack. Encrypted traffic, for instance, cannot be examined for the presence of malware. There is the concept of the "zero-day" worm: malware that attacks a previously unknown

vulnerability and thus would not be detectable. To counter such custom or brand-new "threats of the hour," other technologies have to be
deployed using more sophisticated methods of detection.

This concept, a secure network, would effectively block espionage
of the type experienced by many U.S. research labs and government
agencies around the world, where hackers, either independent or state
sponsored, have broken in through the network and pilfered e-mail,
documents, and databases. Mr. Espy would be thwarted, unless he
turned to more sophisticated attacks.

Second Principle of Simple Security: Good Endpoint Security Assumes the Network Is Hostile

Most organizations have invested heavily in endpoint protection. Over
90 percent of all computers in businesses and government are based
on the Windows operating system. Thanks to widespread outbreaks of
viruses, spyware, and worms, these computers have to be protected or
they quickly become so infected with crud they become inoperable.
These infections are part of everyday computing life in a Microsoft
environment, part of the reason that Linux and other operating systems based on flavors of Unix are gaining traction with sophisticated
computer users (yes, call them geeks). Apple's OSX is based on BSD,
an early type of Unix, and Ubuntu is an open source desktop platform
based on Linux. While non-Windows platforms have less security
maintenance associated with them due to a lack of worms, viruses, and
spyware, they are no more protected against targeted attacks by knowledgeable spies than is Windows.

The key to defending Windows platforms is a constant patching
cycle supported by Microsoft. The second Tuesday of every month
Microsoft issues patches for bugs and vulnerabilities. Those computers
whose owners have enabled automatic updates download and install
these patches on a schedule determined by Microsoft. It is important
to study the consequences of the Microsoft patch cycle, which is a cou-
pling of network services (downloads of patches over the Internet or
from an internal server) with the endpoint.

In October of 2008, Microsoft announced a serious vulnerability
in an obscure service that most Windows platforms contained called
RPC DCOM (Remote Procedure Call–Distributed Component Object
Model). Because the vulnerability was closely related to one announced

on July 17, 2003, that led to the development of MS Blaster, one of the most devastating worms ever, security researchers immediately began warning that it was critical to patch it as quickly as possible. MS Blaster spread from computer to computer over ports 139, 135, 445, and 593. But by 2003 most organizations had learned their lesson and had been forced through expediency to block unused ports with their firewalls. Let us turn to the infamous SQL Slammer worm to understand how this practice of blocking unused ports finally became commonplace. Then we will return to MS Blaster.

History of Worms

There are high points in the constant ebb and flow of vulnerabilities, exploits, and self-replicating worms that can be examined to gain an understanding of the modern state of the security ecology. The first worm was named for the son of an ATT researcher, Robert T. Morris Sr., who wrote a paper in 1985 that exposed a fundamental vulnerability in how computers trusted source IP addresses. His son, Robert Morris Jr., attending Cornell at the time, wrote a piece of code as a proof of concept of his father's theory. The worm was released from an MIT lab November 2, 1988, and infected thousands of Unix machines connected to what was then the government and university specialized network called the Internet. Robert Morris Jr. was prosecuted and sentenced to three years' probation and 400 hours community service for his rash experiment that announced the dawn of the age of network-transmitted malware.

In the ensuing years thousands of worms and viruses were created. Many of the earlier outbreaks were motivated by an anti-Windows sentiment harbored by hackers. They wanted to demonstrate the dangers of using Windows and felt the best way to warn people against adapting to a Microsoft monoculture of "Windows everywhere" was to demonstrate these dangers directly. But, as the Internet became commercialized the motivation for writing malware became commercial as well.

Even with the rapid rise of malware most organizations did little to defend themselves beyond installing anti-virus software on desktops. As the Internet exploded into the communication and commercial phenomenon of the late 1990s, organizations scrambled to deploy Web servers so that they could participate in the so-called new economy of the dot com boom. Capitalizing on the mad rush to "webify," Microsoft created Web server software called Internet Information Server (IIS). Organizations that were already embracing Microsoft's server plat-forms (moving away from Unix and mainframes) quickly deployed Internet facing Web servers based on IIS. In the fall of 2001 Microsoft announced a patch for a serious vulnerability in IIS. At the time Micro-soft had yet to move to the monthly patch release schedule and would issue each new security patch as it became available. Servers that are accessed by end users over networks cannot easily be patched quickly. The typical process is for the IT department to patch a standard con-figuration server in their labs to make sure the patch does not break their applications in some way, then to stage the updates to a server that mirrors the production server, and then finally to update the pro-duction server, usually late at night on a weekend to avoid impacting customers or users. Because patching was so labor intensive and expen-sive, most organizations would either patch on a protracted schedule or not patch at all.

Hackers quickly developed exploits that could give them complete control of any unpatched IIS server connected to the Internet. All the way up to May of 2001 there was a rash of defacements executed by individuals against websites. And, as we saw in chapter 2, the IIS vul-nerability was exploited by Chinese hackers. In May, someone created a self-replicating worm that would spread from vulnerable IIS server to vulnerable IIS server. The worm was called CodeRed. It automated the exploit so that the hacker could have his pick of servers to deface, load additional software on, or use to penetrate further into networks behind firewalls.

Even the fast spread of CodeRed did not force all organizations to improve their patching process. That was demonstrated by Nimda (Ad-min spelled backward). First detected at 9:15 AM September 18, 2001 (one week to the minute after the first passenger plane struck the World Trade Center in New York City), Nimda was a multiheaded worm. It had code that used five vectors to spread. Like CodeRed, it spread from vulnerable IIS server to vulnerable IIS server over the Internet. It also was aware of a special "back door" left behind by CodeRed that would allow an attacker to regain access to an IIS server even after it had been patched (thus the need to completely rebuild infected machines). Nimda also contained code that would exploit a vulnerability in Micro-soft's Web browser, Internet Explorer (IE), to infect anyone who viewed Web pages hosted by a Nimda-infected Web server. Once installed on a desktop Windows machine, Nimda would attempt to spread using open file shares within the organization, installing itself on file servers. It would also spread by exploiting a vulnerability in Microsoft Outlook by sending e-mails, with exploit code attached, to each user's address book. The five-pronged attack vectors of Nimda caused havoc that network security administrators still recall with, "I remember exactly what I was doing when Nimda struck."

The damage caused by Nimda and the amount of lost information has never been quantified. The positive effect of Nimda was to send a wakeup call to every organization to begin to get a grip on the patch issue. Today, thanks in part to Microsoft's improved infrastructure for delivering patches to hundreds of millions of consumer machines and enterprise update servers, to the regular cycle of Patch Tuesday they inaugurated in October 2003, and third-party patch management solutions, most IT departments do a good job of patching.

One more worm must be discussed to shed full light on the evolution of security defenses over the last decade. SQL Slammer was the most virulent self-replicating worm ever. There are several factors that led to its success, if the term success can be applied to a worm that halted the workings of the entire Internet for twelve hours.

SQL Slammer attacked a vulnerability in Microsoft's database server software, SQL. By January of 2003 it was becoming apparent that all of the powerful ways that computers could communicate with each other had to be blocked at network gateways. Remote procedure calls, for instance, were built into Windows platforms so that the marvel of the network could be used to execute code remotely from a central management console. At one point it was common practice for administrators to e-mail everyone in the organization executable code in the form of an attachment. It is hard to believe today that software that would execute without even requiring the e-mail recipient to open the attachment was once considered an important capability for system administrators. It is a recurring theme in the history of cyber security that such naïveté prevails until some exploit demonstrates its folly.

One way in which computers communicate is through database queries. The most common architecture for Web applications is a front-end Web server and a back-end database that manages data and content. Assuming that the firewalls allow it, it is possible to execute a database query across any network using SQL protocols over port 1434. Typically you would never want to leave these ports open because an attacker could attempt to run unauthorized requests against the database, such as "send me the column of credit card numbers stored in the customer database."

SQL Slammer was a very small payload of 376 bytes. It was released late Friday, January 25, 2003. It exploited a previously announced vulnerability in any instance of Microsoft SQL Server that it encountered, infected that machine, and immediately began to spew payloads containing itself. If a vulnerable server were connected to the Internet that evening it became infected. SQL Slammer spread to 80,000 machines in less than ten minutes. It turned every infected machine into a fire hose of internet traffic. Bandwidth utilization on the Internet backbone surged to capacity. South Korea was one of the hardest hit countries. The ISPs and carriers responsible for the backbone scrambled to address this flood. In some cases their networks were so clogged they could not communicate with their edge routers to turn on filters that would block the worm. They had to deploy people to their data centers to access their routers by plugging into the boxes directly or use modems over telephone lines to reset the routers. By noon on the 26th the Internet became functional again. But the world had seen the true potential of the havoc caused by a runaway worm. In retrospect, the author of SQL Slammer displayed commendable caution in releasing it when he did, giving network operators the weekend to respond before financial markets opened Monday morning.

The lesson learned from SQL Slammer was simple: in addition to patching systems, block high-level ports. To this day SQL Slammer often represents the majority of malware traffic on the Internet.

This leads us back to MS Blaster. In July of 2003 Microsoft announced an RPC DCOM vulnerability in just about every Windows platform. Don't forget that at any one time there are many versions of Windows in use around the world. Today there are desktop versions of Windows XP; XP SP1, 2, 3; Vista; Windows 7; Windows Server 2000, 2003, and 2007; as well as various flavors of home PC software and mobile PC software and embedded Windows in industrial controls and medical equipment. Each of these versions is built on some common elements. When an attacker discovers a basic vulnerability in a common component like RPC DCOM, they can write code capable of spreading to the entire family of Windows platforms.

By the summer of 2003 most organizations had begun to block unwanted ports, so when MS Blaster attempted to spread over its special ports they smugly went to bed knowing they were not going to be exposed to it. But, as traveling workers with laptops began to plug in when they came back to work they brought the infection with them. The result was the usual fire drill. Network outages, infected servers, and long hours of cleanup were once again experienced.

There were two possible responses from the security industry to the issue of users bringing infected machines into the network. One solution would be to deploy firewalls and filtering technology internally so that every computer was separated from the core by network security gear. The other response, which is in fact the direction the industry has taken, was to query every endpoint device as it attempted to connect, determine if it had the latest AV signatures and configuration, and only then allow it to connect. This technology, ironically pushed by the largest network security vendor (Cisco, who calls it Network Admission Control, NAC), is deployed most commonly in universities. It violates the principle of decoupling. Rather than simplify, NAC has introduced complications into the network.

From the perspective of fighting espionage, NAC is a panacea, a false cure. Most NAC solutions require the network to trust the report of the very endpoints (laptops, handhelds, etc.) that are in the control of the attacker. No matter what the required configuration or credentials requested, it has been demonstrated that an attacker can spoof them. Of course an attacker can use a completely healthy endpoint to connect to a network and steal data. Our Izzy Espy could use an approved laptop and his credentials as a contractor or employee to attack the network. That is when data protection comes in to play.

Third Principle of Simple Security:
Secure Data Assumes the User Is Hostile

Thus we come to the third principle that will be called into play to defend against espionage. Espionage is, after all, the stealing of data. Protecting data from being stolen requires endpoint and network security as well as specific data and application defenses. The idea is to restrict who has access to particular data and what they can do with that data.

Encryption is the most powerful way to keep data secret. When there are two parties that have to share a document or a message they can choose to encrypt it when they transmit it via e-mail, Instant Message, or even by voice. If a spy manages to intercept the transmission he will not be able to decrypt it. Unfortunately the case of two individuals sharing a secret is a very small subset of all the uses of data. Usually many people have access to data that could be construed as secret. When they are reading a document or storing it to a thumb drive it is unencrypted. If the attacker has access to their computer or is logged in as them, the attacker can see and steal the data.

Access controls can be used to limit the number of people who can get on a network, use certain applications, or see particular directories or databases. Most of the time this is accomplished by requiring user names and passwords to login. Username-password pairs are ineffective against data theft because of the plausible deniability issue. A trusted insider could easily steal another user's account and login, or simply claim that someone else had stolen their ID when confronted with evidence of their actions.

There is another glaring issue within most organizations that poses a significant opportunity for the attacker: privileged accounts.

Privileged accounts are convenient shortcuts. There are two major categories: privileged accounts owned by administrators and those accounts used by programs or servers to communicate with one another. Rather than deal with the complexity of passing login credentials for every authorized user back to the database server, you create one super user, the Web server, and allow it to make any query with rudimentary logging at the database server. For server administration there is a similar short cut. Multiple people on multiple shifts need to get access to servers to back them up, reboot them, patch them, and so forth. It is easier to create one super user account that everyone uses for those tasks. What you end up with is no accountability, no logging of individual behavior, no control. You grant plausible deniability to anyone who abuses those access privileges. Perhaps one of the biggest concerns is privileged account access for databases. Database administrators have to do so many tasks on their servers, from maintaining them to manipulating the data in their stores, that it is extremely cumbersome to ask them to have unique passwords for different tasks. After all, they know the user name and password of the Web server that has to access that database. So even if you give them individual accounts they still login with the elevated credentials of the Web server. Getting a grip on the privileged user account is one of the key challenges in securing an environment from the attacker who has stolen credentials.

Strong authentication has to be deployed. Strong authentication uses two forms of identification. It has become commonplace to issue tokens or smart cards to every user or customer. Tokens display a new string of numbers every minute that they are used to login. Only the person holding the token can see the current number and use it to login. Or the equivalent of a traditional key can be issued in the form of a smart card that has to be swiped in a reader before access is granted. Using the same card for building access would be one of the few physical protections from spying that the IT department can be responsible for.

Information classification is usually the first task for a team trying to implement good data protection. But deciding what is critical data and what is not can be insurmountably difficult. From the perspective of our foreign agent Mr. Espy, data classification does not matter. While classifying credit cards and personally identifiable information such as birth date, social security numbers, and health records may be needed to comply with regulations and standards, it really is not going to help fight cyber espionage, because the attacker is after all the information. Countering espionage must take a comprehensive view of controlling all access to all data to be effective.

When dealing with spies the fear is not about lost data such as stolen laptops or misplaced CDs and thumb drives being accidentally exposed to the wrong eyes. It is that spies can include trusted insiders. Mr. Espy, if his mandate is extended by his employer, could decide that bribery or trickery is called for. He could induce an insider to copy data onto a thumb drive, ipod, or CD and ship it to him. Therefore, device management systems need to be deployed that monitor, alert, or even block the transfer of data to connected devices.

The most effective way to counter the threat posed by insiders is to monitor their activity. Just as closed circuit cameras are used to enforce honesty on the part of bank tellers and casino employees that handle lots of cash, activity monitoring can convince trusted insiders that they will be caught if they abscond with data.

SUMMARY

Have we thwarted our spy? Let's see. Mr. Espy finds all of the publicly accessible data on the target's Web servers and database servers is encrypted and needs strong authentication to access. All of the servers have been patched against everything but a zero-day exploit. He cannot scan internal networks because the firewalls have blocked all ports. He cannot break through the firewalls by inducing someone to browse to a malicious site and become infected because of the content inspection at the gateway. He cannot guess passwords because they change every sixty seconds. Even if he succeeds in infecting an insider's laptop while the employee is traveling and connected through an insecure network at a hotel or coffee shop, his mission is not helped because that laptop is treated as hostile and hacking activity is blocked as effectively on the office LAN as it is at the Internet gateway. While not completely thwarted, Mr. Espy's task has been made much more difficult. And, thanks to the activity monitoring and alerting that has been deployed, there is some hope that his spying would be detected and a damage assessment can be performed.

Countering espionage must be viewed in the light of a new era in cyber security. Most organizations have not been confronted with frontal cyber attacks against their information, or rather, are not aware that they have been attacked. Every organization has to contemplate this threat and formulate a response that goes beyond the traditional measures that were focused on keeping the computing infrastructure working by rooting out viruses, spam, and adware. The spy is very careful to avoid disrupting anything.

The cyber combatant on the other hand, attempts to cause damage that can further their efforts. In the next chapter we approach defending against Denial of Service attacks, the primary weapon of cyber warfare.

TOPPLING E-MAIL SERVERS

E-mail servers are the very core of modern communications infra-structure. This chapter explores e-mail attacks. The Haephrati Trojan events in Israel and the groundbreaking GhostNet report illuminate the vulnerability of e-mail to intrusion and its use as a tool of cyber espionage.

Never, never, never believe any war will be smooth and easy, or that anyone who embarks on the strange voyage can measure the tides and hurricanes he will encounter.

—Winston Churchill

There's no denying that e-mail is the most prevalent and powerful means of Internet communications. While there are now dozens of ways for people to communicate over the Internet, including Instant Messaging, Skype, Google Voice, Twitter, Facebook, and Internet Relay Chat (IRC), e-mail is still the way we organize our lives, confirm flight reservations, schedule meetings, request information, stay in touch with old friends and children away at college, and even manage our business. Look at what happens at work when the e-mail server crashes. Everyone abandons their desks and congregates in the break room until they can get back to their daily duties of reading, writing, and forwarding e-mail.

From an information standpoint, e-mail represents the richest trove for an attacker. The importance of e-mail has not been overlooked by those engaging in cyber espionage. Britain, France, Germany, the White House, and the U.S. Pentagon have all reported compromises to critical military and government e-mail servers.

We will look at those incursions as well as the revealing methodologies of attack as discovered by researchers at Cambridge University and the University of Toronto in their seminal report on what they termed "GhostNet." But first a short explanation of how e-mail works.

During the drama of O. J. Simpson's trial for murder a former official of the U.S. Justice Department made the comment, "If it was easy to spy on e-mail we would all be reading Marcia Clark's e-mail." Ms. Clark was the prosecutor in the trial and the implication was that she was using e-mail to discuss the case among her team, perhaps revealing key stratagems for use against the defendant. His point was that it was close to impossible to intercept e-mail over the Internet, even in 1995. What an innocent time that was! The last decade of the twentieth century was a time before spam. The ILOVEYOU (2000) and Anna Kournikova (2001) viruses had not been born. The NSA had not tapped into ATT's data center (2005) to sniff the backbone traffic of the Internet and search for key words in the hopes of uncovering terrorist plots. Microsoft products even used e-mail as a way for IT staff to issue commands remotely to desktop computers to install new applications. Just receiving an e-mail from the IT administrators would execute the software they had sent.

E-mail has changed dramatically since those days. According to Barracuda Networks' 2007 Spam Report, nearly 95 percent of all e-mails sent are spam. Viruses, Trojan horses, and worms are propagated through e-mail. E-mail protection has become a big business with dozens of companies offering products and even Web-based services to scrub e-mails of spam and viruses. E-mail archiving and data mining products abound.

How does e-mail work? It is based on a very simple protocol, SMTP, which appropriately stands for Simple Mail Transfer Protocol. When you hit the send button on an e-mail its first stop is at your e-mail server. It could be Gmail, Yahoo Mail, or your ISP or corporate e-mail server. According to SecuritySpace.com, there were over 1.7 million e-mail servers in 2007. Each of them has the same set of tasks: receiving, forwarding, and storing e-mail for pick up. An outgoing e-mail has a recipient's address that indicates the name of the recipient e-mail server. Let's use stiennon@gmail.com as an example. Your e-mail server checks the Domain Name System (DNS) to find the location of the mail server for the gmail.com domain. That is translated into an IP address. Your mail server then contacts the Gmail server and says "Hello, I have an e-mail for recipient 'stiennon.'" If Gmail recognizes the recipient it says "OK send it on," and your e-mail is transmitted via SMTP to Gmail, where it is stored for me to retrieve it. (If you want to contact me I would not advise using my Gmail address. As of this writing I have 66,929 messages in my inbox!)

So for an attacker to intercept your e-mail they need to either be able to:

1. Read your e-mail from your computer
2. Read your e-mail as it is uploaded to your e-mail server
3. Read your e-mail on your e-mail server
4. Read your e-mail as it is transmitted over the Internet to the recipient e-mail server (Gmail)
5. Read it on the Gmail server
6. Compromise the Gmail account

The last possibility was demonstrated during the 2008 U.S. presidential election, when the Gmail account of the Republican candidate for vice president, Sarah Palin, was compromised. At one time cracking e-mail accounts was a trivial task that involved setting up a program (Jack the Ripper was one such) and trying every possible password using a so-called dictionary attack. Most e-mail services now lock an attacker out after too many failed password attempts. This does not stop a clever attacker who uses publicly available information about the target to guess a password. Of course the first passwords to try are the word "password" or "123456." A keystroke logger loaded on your computer will record your password as well. And then there is shoulder surfing. An accomplished cyber assailant can watch your fingers as they type and "read" every keystroke.

Password attacks work against just about any e-mail account at an ISP, and often against corporate e-mail servers. The attacker just needs to be armed with your name, e-mail address (which identifies the mail server!), and maybe your birth date, spouse's birth date and name, and your favorite sports team to make some intelligent guesses about your password.

Attacking individual e-mail accounts is a refined art, but the most valuable achievement is gaining control of the e-mail server itself. If an attacker has the same rights as the administrator of the e-mail server he can create e-mail accounts, get password files (encrypted but crackable using tools like L0phtcrack), read e-mails that are in the queue for pickup or delivery, read the logs, intercept e-mail, and even modify e-mails in transit. An attacker could easily run code that would forward copies of every desired e-mail to their own account somewhere else.

Imagine the critical knowledge that could be obtained by an attacker who compromised the e-mail server of the prosecuting attorney's office, the opposing candidate in a presidential election, the prime minister or president of a country, the office of the Dalai Lama, or the Joint Chiefs of the U.S. Armed Forces. Beyond pure espionage, imagine the mischief that could be caused if e-mails could be sent from individual accounts on those servers with completely false messages.

The growing importance of e-mail communication has been accompanied by more and more sophisticated attacks against e-mail. Corporate competitive intelligence-gathering and state-sponsored espionage teams find rich targets of opportunity within e-mail accounts.

China does not discriminate in selecting its targets for cyber espionage. The list of countries that have reported evidence of Chinese sleuthing and successful penetrations of their critical assets now includes the UK, France, Germany, Australia, and India.

In September of 2007, the UK reported that China had successfully taken over e-mail servers at Whitehall, the administrative seat of government including the Foreign Office and the Ministry of Defense. An article published at the time reports:

> Security and defence officials are coy about what they know of specific attacks. However, they say several Whitehall departments have fallen victim to China's cyberwarriors. One expert described it as a "constant ongoing problem."[1]

In May of 2007, German intelligence officials announced that they had discovered Trojan horse software installed on computers in the offices of the German chancellery as well as the foreign, economy, and research ministries:

The so-called "Trojan" espionage programs were concealed in Microsoft Word documents and PowerPoint files which infected IT installations when opened, SPIEGEL reported. Information was taken from German computers in this way on a daily basis by hackers based in the northwestern province of Lanzhou, Canton province and Beijing. German officials believe the hackers were being directed by the People's Liberation Army and that the programs were redirected via computers in South Korea to disguise their origin.[2]

Despite promises by the Chinese government to investigate these incidents fully, a 2009 article in *Spiegel Online* reports:

Each year, special virus scanners detect about 600 attempts to insert sophisticated spy software into the two central Internet interfaces of IVBB, a computer network that links the computers at the German Chancellery with government ministries in Bonn and Berlin.[3]

In response to the announcements by Germany, the UK, and the United States, France revealed that it, too, was under cyber attack emanating from China:

"We have indications that our information systems were the object of attacks, like in the other countries," the secretary-general of national defense (SGDN) Francis Delon said, confirming a report published in the French newspaper *Le Monde*.[4]

While 2007 witnessed a flood of reports of attacks on these government information resources, there are more recent reports:

According to an internal Department of Foreign Affairs and Trade briefing, a fake email was sent to a number of DFAT officers in the week beginning July 12, just over a week after the arrest in China of Rio Tinto executive Stern Hu.

The fake email purported to be sent from what the DFAT briefing described as "a senior Commonwealth Public Service officer" and had the subject heading "Australia-China Free Trade Agreement Negotiations Update."

After examination of the suspicious email, DFAT's diplomatic security branch issued an urgent warning to all staff that such emails could contain "dangerous [electronic] viruses which could extract information from user desktops or disrupt their operations."[5]

The summer of 2008 saw some interesting revelations from the White House and the Obama and McCain campaigns. All had had their e-mail servers compromised. The *Financial Times* reported on November 8, 2008:

> Chinese hackers have penetrated the White House computer network on multiple occasions, and obtained e-mails between government officials, a senior US official told the *Financial Times.*[6]

And *Newsweek* reported that after concerns over what the Obama campaign thought were phishing attacks:

> both the FBI and the Secret Service came to the campaign with an ominous warning: "You have a problem way bigger than what you understand," an agent told Obama's team. "You have been compromised, and a serious amount of files have been loaded off your system." The following day, Obama campaign chief David Plouffe heard from White House chief of staff Josh Bolten, to the same effect: "You have a real problem . . . and you have to deal with it." The Feds told Obama's aides in late August that the McCain campaign's computer system had been similarly compromised. A top McCain official confirmed to NEWSWEEK that the campaign's computer system had been hacked and that the FBI had become involved.[7]

Later, the Obama campaign said there was evidence that they had been attacked from China.

All of these revelations have been met with vehement denials of Chinese government involvement despite the digital trail left behind that led back to servers in China, sometimes staged in South Korea, just as Shawn Carpenter had discovered. Plausible deniability is a key factor in cyber espionage, just as it can be used in the more aggressive cases of massive denial of service attacks discussed in later chapters. Available published reports quote Western officials who say they have evidence of Chinese People's Liberation Army involvement but those must be weighed against the abject denials from Beijing. That changed in March 2009.

Researchers in Toronto and Canada have investigated and reported on a worldwide network of compromised machines they dub Ghost-Net. Their investigation produced the first public reports that tie the Chinese government directly to cyber espionage. Attribution in cyberwar is the most difficult aspect of defense. Inaccurate attribution of the principals in a cyber act of aggression could lead to disastrous repercussions. Yet, in April 2009, researchers in Cambridge, supported by a team at the University of Toronto, the Munk Institute, and researchers in Tibet published the results of their investigation into targeted espionage against the office of the Dalai Lama.

Thanks to this research we can understand the methodologies that are used by Chinese operatives to compromise e-mail servers and winnow their way into the networks and operations of the Pentagon, Whitehall, and other targets, techniques that are almost impossible to counter with accepted best practices in network and host security.

China's repression of Tibet is well known to the millions of citizens of Tibet as well as the watching world. The greatest threat to Chinese hegemony in their vast territories is the pacifist Dalai Lama, a spiritual leader who has been living in exile since he fled the invading Chinese Red Army in 1959. His teachings and the activities of a worldwide Tibetan liberation movement could have cascading consequences that eventually topple Communist rule in Tibet. Thus it is not surprising that China would seek to infiltrate the operations of the Dalai Lama's global organization.

In late 2008 a researcher at the University of Cambridge, Dr. Shishir Nagaraja, was contacted by members of the Dalai Lama's office in Dharamsala, a city in India across the border from Tibet where the Tibetan government-in-exile resides. Dr. Nagaraja had worked with them as an intern and because of his interest in IT security they approached him with their problem. The monks suspected that their critical e-mails were not safe. Two incidents fueled that suspicion.

The first incident occurred when the Dalai Lama's office sent an e-mail to a number of diplomats requesting their presence at an upcoming meeting. Before they could place a follow-up call the next morning one of the recipients of that e-mail had received a call from the Chinese government warning him not to attend the meeting. The most likely way the Chinese government could have known about the meeting was to have intercepted that e-mail.

The second incident was spookier. The Dalai Lama's office also uses the Internet to promote its message of peace. An organization in Tibet called Drewla employs a team of "social influencers" whose task is to engage Tibetan and Chinese citizens in dialogue online to educate and spread the Dalai Lama's word. By leaving positive comments on blogs and using Instant Messaging they seek to counter the Chinese propaganda that the Dalai Lama is an evil force for counterrevolutionary action. One such woman who engaged in these positive messaging activities crossed the border into Tibet and was arrested. She was confronted with two years' worth of IM communications and was incarcerated for two months of interrogation. The GhostNet researchers concluded that the Drewla organization's computers had been compromised.

These and other suspicious events led the Dalai Lama's office to reach out to Dr. Nagaraja at the University of Cambridge. Recognizing the importance of researching cyber espionage activities that were attributable to China, Dr. Nagaraja got on the case. He arranged to travel to Dharamsala and investigate. His first step was to put a sniffer on the network of the Dalai Lama's office.

A sniffer is a software package that captures all of the IP packets that cross a particular network segment. The software can be installed on a laptop and when the laptop is plugged in to the network it starts recording and analyzing all of the network traffic it sees. In this case Nagaraja used the free open source software called WireShark. Sure enough, machines on the internal network of the office of the Dalai Lama were sending messages to IP addresses that were apparently in China. Those IP addresses could be traced to China's Xinjiang Uyghur Autonomous Region, where police and intelligence units dealing with Tibetan independence campaigners are based, according to his research.

Armed with those initial findings, Nagaraja realized he needed help. As we have seen with Shawn Carpenter, some types of computer investigations are deemed outside the law in some countries. The UK in particular has laws that make these types of investigations problematic. So Nagaraja contacted his one-time mentor and the founder of the HoneyNet project, Rafal Rohozinski, who had established the SecDev Group, which worked with the Munk Centre of Trinity College, at the University of Toronto. Rohozinski was the right person to contact. While engaged with British intelligence operations he had been stationed in Eastern Europe and was very familiar with spy trade craft.

Rohozinski's team, the SecDev Group, included Greg Walton, a researcher who had spent considerable time in India, and Nart Villenueve, who had conducted the important research that revealed that the Chinese ISP TOM had modified Skype, the popular free messaging and voice communication software, to intercept and record all communication containing key words or from key usernames. This team jumped on the case.

Cyber investigations involve piecing together many strings of data in the hopes of finding connections. Starting with the data available on a single network or infected computer, an investigator finds him or herself following multiple threads down multiple paths. Tools employed in a researcher's investigation can include written notebooks, spreadsheets, and a computer's directory system for holding captured files. The Munk researchers recognized that they could use the enhanced functionality of a tool being developed at Palantir Technologies in Palo Alto, California. This project was the beginning of a partnership with Palantir, who needed the Munk researchers' expert input on what the tool should do to enhance a cyber researcher's capabilities.

A side note on Palantir Technologies. Walk to the end of University Avenue in downtown Palo Alto, California. Just before you have to cross El Camino Real and enter the campus of Stanford University, turn left one block. You will find a three-story office building surrounding an atrium that contains the usual Silicon Valley start-ups and venture capital firms. Palantir has grown in just five years to a team of 150. Their office space has already spilled beyond the few rooms that had once housed Google when it too was a start-up. Alex Karp created Palantir to commercialize capabilities that had been developed by one of his backers, a founder of PayPal. PayPal, the payment processing service now owned by eBay, had to counter continuous attacks from hackers, scam artists, and fraudulent users. They developed correlation software that would identify suspicious activity. Post-9-11, Alex recognized the importance of that correlation technology and founded Palantir to help the Department of Homeland Security and law enforcement officials to track disparate data that could lead to the discovery of terrorist activity. Working with the SecDev, team Palantir would be able to expand the use of their product to cyber investigators.

Shawn Carpenter recognized that an IP address that was the source of attacks against Sandia had also been implicated in earlier attacks against Lockheed Martin. That amazing ability to recognize an IP address first seen months before is something that security researchers get good at. But researchers using Palantir's technology would see correlations like that instantly. Data that had been gathered months before would be correlated with new data as it was gathered and key connections would be made and highlighted graphically for the analyst.

Anatomy of an Attack on E-mail Infrastructure.
Let us look at the entire process used by those attacking the Dalai Lama's office. The scary aspect is that the techniques used do not require sophisticated network attack capabilities. Completely secure e-mail servers and networks can be compromised very simply.

An attacker identifies members of a target organization by reading public discussion forums, news items, even blogs. Even if e-mail addresses are not posted it is fairly easy to determine them once a name is known. Just e-mail an innocuous spam message, advertising Viagra for instance, to every possible combination of first and last name at the organization's domain. John Smith could be jsmith@, john.smith@, john-smith@ or even jsmith123@. The e-mail server will usually bounce e-mails to addresses that do not exist. By a process of elimination the attacker can determine the correct e-mail address. If a standard format such as firstname.lastname is used it just makes the job easier for the attackers.

The next step is to send a carefully crafted e-mail that appears to come from someone with legitimate information or business with a file attached to it. The attachment might be what it claims to be, a white paper, presentation, or job offer. But, it also contains the Trojan horse, which installs itself when the attachment is opened and starts to capture everything the target types as well as files from her machine. This level of access makes it easy to grab the username and password for the target's e-mail, which could be stored on the computer or would be captured when it was typed in. After that, e-mails can be sent from that person's internal e-mail address and the rest of the organization can be compromised. If the e-mail administrator's PC becomes infected, the attackers can log in to the e-mail server as the administrator and do further damage. They can replace legitimate attachments with their malware. The Snooping Dragon report contains an example of such an e-mail.

Imagine the damage and confusion that could be caused if message content were changed as well!

The SecDev team, using Palantir's product to keep track of their investigation, dived in.

The first step was to investigate the compromised machines within the Dalai Lama's organization. They were able to identify the Trojan horse software used and discover the control servers that it communicated with to get updates, change where they reported to, and to which they uploaded stolen files.

Four of these servers were discovered. And, just as Shawn Carpenter uncovered an extensive cyber espionage effort called Titan Rain that targeted several U.S. research, military, and commercial networks, the SecDev researchers discovered GhostNet.

The GhostNet is over 1,200 machines throughout the world that receive commands and upload data to those four servers. The GhostNet report states:

> Close to 30% of the infected computers can be considered high-value and include the ministries of foreign affairs of Iran, Bangladesh, Latvia, Indonesia, Philippines, Brunei, Barbados and Bhutan; embassies of India, South Korea, Indonesia, Romania, Cyprus, Malta, Thailand, Taiwan, Portugal, Germany and Pakistan; the ASEAN (Association of Southeast Asian Nations) Secretariat, SAARC (South Asian Association for Regional Cooperation), and the Asian Development Bank; news organizations; and an unclassified computer located at NATO headquarters.

> The *GhostNet* system directs infected computers to download a Trojan known as *gh0st RAT* that allows attackers to gain complete, *real-time* control. These instances of *gh0st RAT* are consistently controlled from commercial Internet access accounts located on the island of Hainan, People's Republic of China.

The report does not mention the fact that gh0st RAT is a software package developed and maintained by Chinese hackers.

The revelation that there is a group of infected computers placed inside so many offices of diplomats and organizations around the world and controlled by servers within China indicates an orchestrated cyber espionage effort that is apparently segmented. Why, one should ask, were there no U.S. agencies or embassies that were compromised and controlled by these servers? Would Chinese spies ignore the United States? Or, is there another entire network devoted to spying on the United States? Or several?

Other questions can be raised. The Chinese government has responded to every accusation that they engage in cyber espionage with bald denials. Why, in the case of GhostNet did they burn (to use spy lingo) their operation by engaging in activities that could only have been directed by insider knowledge gained through hacking? During World War II the British were very careful to always have a cover story if they used information gleaned from decrypting German High Command traffic. If they ever acted on their knowledge without those cover stories the Germans would have changed their encryption techniques. In the GhostNet case, confronting the Drewla employee with her communications and warning the diplomat away from a meeting revealed that they had compromised the Dalai Lama's e-mail system. Now the Dalai Lama's office, the Free Tibet organization, and as many of the owners of compromised machines as the SecDev team can alert will harden their systems, remove the offending spy programs, and put in place network protections. For that matter why did the attackers leave their network in place after they had burned it?

The Snooping Dragon report published by Nagaraja at the same time as the larger GhostNet report points out the gravity of a situation where people's lives could be put at stake if they are identified with, for instance, organizing schools within Tibet. This puts the infiltration of the Dalai Lama's network at a different level than the competitive intelligence gathering we saw in Israel using Michael Haephrati's Trojan even though the technology used was very similar.

After seeing just how easy it is to compromise e-mail, networks, and e-mail servers, would it be surprising to learn that China has been implicated in an attack on the core of the U.S. Department of Defense, the e-mail servers of the Pentagon?

THE PENTAGON

Far from secure, the U.S. military is demonstrated to be particularly vulnerable. In this chapter we discuss the direct attacks on the U.S. Pentagon and infiltration of critical systems in the defense supply chain and theater operations.

> *There is no security on this earth; there is only opportunity.*
>
> —Douglas MacArthur

On September 11, 2001, at 9:38 AM, American Airlines Flight 77 crashed into the Pentagon with a full load of Jet Fuel #1. The conflagration killed the crew, 60 passengers, and 125 military and civilian personnel in the Pentagon. The first violence against the center of all U.S. military operations caused $150 million in damages. The Department of Defense used the occasion of rebuilding the damaged structure to invest in revamping the network infrastructure of the Pentagon. By 2003, they embarked on a revamping of systems and networks including security.

At 3,705,793 square feet, the Pentagon is one of the largest office complexes in the world. It houses 23,000 military and civilian personnel who direct the operations of the 1.4 million strong U.S. Defense

Department. It has been the center of the DOD since it was built in 1943, in the middle of World War II. In 1989, the U.S. Congress approved a Department of Defense initiative to completely renovate the Pentagon over a period of approximately 12 years. The goal was to create an "intelligent building." Unfortunately "intelligent" referred to HVAC controls, not to its networks.

A naïve outside observer would have assumed that the center of command and control of the supreme military machine in the world would have the best security. This was not the case in 2003. As in many government institutions that grow and expand with time, the networks in the Pentagon were a hodgepodge of technology and conflicting jurisdictions. There were over 20 separate networks administrated by separate groups within the U.S. military: the army, the navy, the Joint Chiefs of Staff, and so forth.

The Pentagon had adopted an IP network in 1995 soon after the Internet had been officially released from its research-only status. By 2003 there were thousands of network devices, desktop computers, and servers, including e-mail servers, that provided the computing infrastructure of an enormous military nexus.

But universities and many branches of the U.S. government continued the principles of academic freedom on which the Internet was founded. This philosophy of "academic freedom" is an anachronism, an undocumented extension of the First Amendment guarantee of free speech. It holds that because researchers are publicly funded the results of their research should be freely available and also that limiting access to information is a restriction of a researcher's right to free and easy academic exploration. With our perspective of little over a decade it is already hard to imagine a time when government and universities, even commercial entities, connected to the Internet with no security at all; no firewalls, no intrusion prevention, no patch management, no anti-virus and no anti-spyware. Yet, they did.

The Internet has had adoption rates that exceeded those of the telegraph, telephone, or television in previous eras, it has also led to a security nightmare for the Department of Defense that may be impossible to correct. Within the Pentagon, multiple network jurisdictions have multiple connections to other military networks, and the Internet, through many points. It is a snarled ball of yarn that can only be sorted out with a pair of scissors.

Because the Pentagon represents the core of military operations for the United States, has many disparate networks, conflicting management hierarchies, and houses computer servers for command and control, it also represents the most desirable target for cyber intelligence-gathering and even cyber attack.

In the summer of 2003, even after the experience of multiple worms such as CodeRed, Nimda, and SQL Slammer, the Pentagon still had little ability to detect and block those worms, let alone a targeted attack. The primary line of defense was a firewall backed up by IDS technology: Intrusion Detection Systems. The same technology that Shawn Carpenter was busy maintaining at the time in Albuquerque, IDS was already falling out of favor in the industry because it was completely passive, doing nothing to stop attacks, only alerting users about them. The Pentagon, in July of 2003, was preparing to spend over $100 million on commercial IDS products to replace or enhance the open source freeware they had deployed.

It has to be pointed out that in 2003 the Pentagon was investing in their own ability to carry out investigations after the fact in the same manner that Clifford Stoll did at Berkeley Labs in 1988, and Shawn Carpenter did at Sandia Labs. The difficulty with IDS systems though is that they generate thousands, sometimes millions, of alerts based on suspicious network events everyday. Sorting through them and determining what happened is difficult and expensive. In an ideal world the Pentagon would have been concentrating on deploying patch management capabilities, internal firewalls, IPS (Intrusion Prevention Systems), and access controls. But, because of the infighting between groups and the helter-skelter growth of its networks and topologies the Pentagon focused on perimeter firewalls and network monitoring.

We have already seen that the NISSC in London warned two years later that massive concentrated attacks had been emanating from the "Far East" from at least 2003 on. China had learned much since May 2001, and was continuing, albeit still maintaining a shield of denial.

Gary McKennon was one of many hackers who targeted U.S. defense networks over the years. In 2001 and 2002 he successfully breached over 100 computers in the Pentagon and elsewhere using simple password guessing tools. He is a strange character who claims he was looking for (and found!) evidence of the U.S. military's cover-up of interactions with aliens. If nothing else, his success demonstrates the low level of security protections put in place by the U.S. government agencies in the not-too-recent past.

In June 2007, U.S. Defense Secretary Robert Gates admitted that e-mail servers in the Pentagon had been compromised leading to those systems' being taken off-line and the disruption of internal communication within the Pentagon. He downplayed the seriousness of the attacks, claiming that only low-level personnel were affected. Yet 1,500 computers were taken off-line to address the issue. To this date the length of time that the e-mail servers were compromised has not been revealed. During that time an attacker would have had access to information that could have posed a significant national security threat. Analysis of those e-mails, even if they were from low-level personnel would have provided important intelligence to an attacker even if it was about mundane things like day-to-day operations.

In July 2007, General Wesley Clark reported to a Congressional committee investigating the dangers of peer-to-peer networks that data from the Pentagon had made its way onto LimeWire, a file-sharing service. His testimony included that an investigator had found:

> The entire Pentagon's secret backbone network infrastructure diagram, including the server and IP addresses, with password transcripts for Pentagon's secret network servers, the Department of Defense employees' contact information, secure sockets layer instructions, and certificates allowing access to the disclosing contractors' IT systems, and ironically, a letter from OMB which explicitly talks about the risks associated with P2P file-sharing networks.

The data had been on a Pentagon contractor's computer at home. LimeWire, sitting on that computer, automatically made it available to other computers on its network and therefore available to anyone who might be looking for it and was also on the LimeWire peer-to-peer network.

At a conference in April 2009 Pentagon officials claimed they had spent over $100 million to clean up after cyber incursions in the prior six months. That is an astronomical number even for a large organization like the Pentagon and it is an indication of massive incursions.

And on April 21, 2009, the *Wall Street Journal* reported that since at least 2007 intruders had been harvesting design data on the Pentagon's most expensive project ever, the $300 billion Joint Strike Fighter, the F-35 Lightning II. The *Journal* said that six former and current Defense Department officials confirmed that the fighter program had been breached. The assailants encrypted several terabytes (thousands of gigabytes) of data they found and siphoned it off the Defense nonclassified network (NIPRNet), a methodology reminiscent of that observed by Shawn Carpenter during the Titan Rain episode of 2005. Quoting the article:

> Investigators traced the penetrations back with a "high level of certainty" to known Chinese Internet protocol, or IP, addresses and digital fingerprints that had been used for attacks in the past, said a person briefed on the matter.[1]

While there are several nations that would go to this level of effort to steal design data, China is often the suspect because of its history of stealing technology for both industrial and military purposes. The most famous incident was China's development of a small thermonuclear warhead suitable for delivery via Intercontinental Ballistic Missile (ICBM) that leveraged data stolen from the massive investment the United States had made in technology. The stolen design data gave China what they needed to develop a compact method of focusing the output of a nuclear fission explosion to ignite the fusion reaction in an H-bomb. (The U.S. warhead is called the W-88.)

In his annual testimony to the House Permanent Select Committee on Intelligence on February 7, 2008, J. Michael McConnell, the Director of National Intelligence, failed to mention the loss of information about the Joint Strike Fighter. He did say:

> We assess that nations, including Russia and China, have the technical capabilities to target and disrupt elements of the US information infrastructure and for intelligence collection. Nation states and criminals target our government and private sector information networks to gain competitive advantage in the commercial sector.

And in November 2008, reports circulated that the U.S. Defense Department, in particular its Central Command and military operations in Afghanistan and Iraq, were under attack from Russian sources. Computers in combat zones were affected. At least one classified network was reported compromised.

The agent for this attack was the USB-born worm w32.agent.btz. According to F-Secure, the worm is installed from an infected thumb drive and places itself on every drive on a computer including any USB drive that is attached to it. The worm connected to a server that the domain-tracking service Netcraft reported was in Hong Kong, but the domain itself was registered in Christmas Island domain: worldnews.ath.cx.

These series of events, from the crazy young hackers of a decade ago to the bulk exfiltration of fighter plane data, to a targeted malware attack that affected computers in war zones, have created a dramatic shift in thinking within the militaries of the world. As we will see in chapter 14, changes are accelerating within defense organizations. The U.S. Defense Department in particular has awakened to its vulnerability to cyber attack.

GEOPOLITICAL CYBER HOT SPOTS

In this chapter we discuss conflicts around the world that are taking on a cyber element. Computer networks and attacks across them lend themselves to asymmetric warfare. Even the smallest country or terrorist organization can use cyberwar to its advantage.

The secret of war lies in the communications.

—Napoleon Bonaparte

While the great powers are actively engaged in studying cyber warfare and reorganizing their military hierarchies to accommodate a new battleground, the real innovation in orchestrating cyber attacks is occurring in regional conflicts between opposing nations. One complication in studying cyberwar is the involvement of organized crime, such as is evident in Russia, and terrorist organizations that could benefit in many ways from wielding cyber weapons. Opponents in this warfare may not be states, but opposing ethnic or religious groups.

By watching developments globally one can learn of the advance of cyber attack techniques as well as measures to be taken to ward them off.

A map of the world that was shaded in colors from cool green, indicating peace, to hot red, indicating conflict, would immediately reveal hot spots worth watching for evidence of cyberwar. Overlaying that map with one that indicates levels of network connectivity would further highlight certain areas. Certainly the border between the United States and Canada, two of the most network savvy regions, would be a pleasantly bucolic green. There may be hot spots in several areas of Africa, but the seemingly constant atrocities occurring there are not enhanced by cyber conflict because those areas are behind the networking curve. A glance at the Middle East would show Israel, highly advanced in networking and technology, lit up like a beacon. It is the center of a war of ideologies and an area to watch for cyber warfare developments. Further east you would probably pass over the geopolitical hot spots of Saudi Arabia, Afghanistan, Iraq, and Iran, because those societies have not come to rely as heavily on the Internet for lack of technology investment, as well as governments that have restricted the free growth of the Internet and access to information. But wait, perhaps we should dwell a moment on Iran, certainly the world's focus when it comes to potential for development into a hot spot that could engulf the globe as it test-fires mid-range ballistic missiles and continues to refine materials for creating nuclear warheads to arm those missiles.

To the east of Iran an uncomfortably close hot spot glows between Pakistan and India, two contentious states that are already members of the nuclear club and very advanced in their use of technology and the Internet.

Southeast Asia has its share of geopolitical hot spots, as age-old differences between cultures continue to percolate. Let us examine cyber conflict in three worrisome regional disputes: Israel versus Hamas, Syria, and Iran; Pakistan versus India; and North Korea versus South Korea (and the United States). Each of these conflicts is revealing new developments in cyber warfare. Each is being carefully watched by the war-fighting agencies of the world's other states. Surviving cyberwar will require learning from each of these conflicts.

The weapons of cyberwar are far cheaper, and easier, to acquire than an AK-47 assault rifle or the materials to assemble an IED (improvised explosive device). A couple of hours of research online can give any cyber assailant the knowledge and tools needed to launch a denial of service attack or deface a website. This very low cost has disruptive potential equal to the changes wrought in medieval times by arming peasants with pikes to counter cavalry charges or minutemen with muskets to ward off the organized troops of an occupying British army in revolutionary America. This ease of acquisition and use is contributing to the perceived chaos in the myriad hot spots around the world. It is not possible to tie together all cyber conflicts into a cohesive story. Even so there are lessons to be learned from examining each incident. Lessons that have to be learned by modern war fighters and IT security practitioners.

We have seen how cyber conflict is arising in these regions because it is easy, low-cost, and effective at least as far as propaganda and the war of ideas is concerned. The disruption of communications by kinetic attacks on undersea cables has been demonstrated, even though the vehicles for those attacks are dragging anchors and not well-placed charges of C4 explosives or cruise missiles. But the history of cyber conflict in these hot spots is a very short one.

The repercussions of escalation of cyber attacks must be addressed. This book does not delve into potential scenarios of cybergeddon, cyber Katrina, or cyber holocaust. Those exercises are not needed in light of the actual events around the world that drive home the point that cyber war is with us in various forms, governments, and businesses. Individuals have to address the elevated risks to their computing and network resources.

An examination of the history of warfare (as covered in chapter 12) will reveal that the steady increase in the scope of destruction and slaughter that is regrettably part of human history was abruptly curtailed at the end of World War II. The atom bomb and the never-used-in-conflict hydrogen bomb changed the course of history. The consequences of using these ultimate weapons in war have been too horrific for any sane nation to consider unleashing. The delicate balance between the superpowers of the twentieth century was maintained by that sanity and parity in destructive power.

If a government of a nuclear-capable country or group became convinced that they could launch nuclear-tipped missiles at their enemy without suffering a retaliation of the same order, would they? Could a cyber attack disable a country's ability to launch retaliatory missiles? Those are the questions that underlie the importance of defending against cyber attack—questions that far outweigh the temporary power outage or disruption to air traffic control or stock exchanges addressed by most cyber scenarios contemplated to date. Nuclear command and control, as well as power and communication infrastructures, must be made impervious to cyber attack to avoid a destabilization that could lead to nuclear conflict. The cyber arms race that is already arising will revolve around these questions.

It may be shortsighted to limit discussion of hot spots to regions that have nuclear weapons, but it is necessary because of the greater implications for cyberwar in those places, which could upset the tenuous balance of power between nuclear-armed states.

ISRAEL

There are many unsupported accounts of cyber activity on the part of Israeli operatives that position Israel as a master of cyber espionage and infiltration. In November 2009, *Spiegel Online* published the story of the destruction of the Syrian nuclear facility. A senior Syrian official checked into a hotel in London. He was under observation by Mossad, Israel's covert agency. When he left his laptop unattended in his hotel room, the Israelis entered his room and snuck a Trojan horse onto it. *Spiegel Online* reveals that there were many documents exfiltrated from that laptop that proved the existence of a nuclear research facility on Israel's doorstep. Information stolen from this laptop gave Israel evidence of Syria's nuclear research facility including:

> One of the photos showed an Asian in blue tracksuit trousers, standing next to an Arab. The Mossad quickly identified the two men as Chon Chibu and Ibrahim Othman. Chon is one of the leading members of the North Korean nuclear program, and experts believe that he is the chief engineer behind the Yongbyon plutonium reactor. Othman is the director of the Syrian Atomic Energy Commission.[1]

Israel bombed that facility in September 2006, and Syria bulldozed and paved over the remains to hide the evidence.

From a defense industry publication in 2007:

> Elements of the attack included some brute-force jamming, which is still an important element of attacking air defenses, U.S. analysts say. Also, Syrian air defenses are still centralized and dependent on dedicated HF and VHF communications, which made them vulnerable. The analysts don't believe any part of Syria's electrical grid was shut down. They do contend that network penetration involved both remote air-to-ground electronic attack and penetration through computer-to-computer links.

"There also were some higher-level, non-tactical penetrations, either direct or as diversions and spoofs, of the Syrian command-and-control capability, done through network attack," says an intelligence specialist.[2]

It is not surprising to discover that Israel, a technologically advanced country under a state of siege from most of its neighbors, engages in active cyber espionage and disruption.

Israel has been the target of numerous cyber attacks from Islamist groups. The usual scenario is triggered by an event that leads to retaliation that includes defacement of websites, and Distributed Denial of Service (DDoS) attacks.

In January 2009 Israel invaded the Gaza Strip to eliminate the rocket-launching sites that had been terrorizing the nearby communities. The ensuing attacks against Israeli websites including government and hospitals were typical of the type of politically motivated incidents coming from the region.

PAKISTAN AND INDIA

There have been four land wars and numerous skirmishes between Pakistan and India since the post–World War II partitioning that created the two countries. These came to a halt as both sides demonstrated that they had joined the nuclear club. Deterrence, the doctrine of threatening annihilation at the next outbreak of hostilities, apparently works. Because of the differing religious, political, and national views held by both sides it is not surprising that there is an almost constant barrage of Internet attacks against each other's websites and information. Those attacks are probably not state-sponsored but are just hacktivists demonstrating national pride with the tools available to them. Nart Villenueve of *Infowar Monitor* and the Secdev Group (more on Nart in the discussion of GhostNet), analyzed the defacements that were observed leading up to the Mumbai terrorist attacks of November 27, 2008.

On November 17, 2008 the web site of the Oil and Gas Regulatory Authority of Pakistan (OGRA), www.ogra.org.pk, was defaced by an Indian defacement group called Hindu Militant Group (HMG). By November 24, 2008 a Pakistani defacement group called Pakistan Cyber Army (PCA) formed and responded to the defacement and defaced the

web site of India's Oil and Natural Gas Corporation Ltd. (ONGC), www
.ongcindia.com.[3]

Nart points out the sophistication of the Pakistani group in targeting
a website similar to the one the Indian hackers had defaced. The groups
involved in these attacks have since called a truce, which is a good idea
considering the heightened tensions in the region.

NORTH KOREAN ATTACKS, JULY 2009

If ever there was a gnat of a country buzzing around the head of an
elephant it is surely North Korea confronting the United States. North
Korea is a country in the technological dark ages dominated by a despot
who has impoverished its people. It cannot even provide electricity, as
evidenced by grim nighttime satellite images that show a dark blotch
above the demilitarized zone between North Korea and the democratic
South Korea. That said, North Korea has squandered what little resources it has on developing nuclear bombs and the missiles to deliver
them. It is using this capability to garner international attention. The
escalating tensions between North Korea, its democratic neighbor to
the south, and the United States led to the incidents of summer 2009.

Despite agreements to curtail its nuclear program, North Korea deto-
nated an underground atomic bomb on May 25, 2009. The United Nations was quick to respond and passed United Nations Security Council
Resolution 1874 on June 12 with sanctions against providing financial
assistance and permission to search North Korean cargo vessels. North
Korea's response to that external pressure was to escalate its posturing
with a launch of multiple missiles on the weekend of July 4. The choice
of date, U.S. Independence Day, did not go unnoticed, and the United
States even took precautions to prepare to shoot down the missiles if
they approached Hawaii, over 3,000 miles away.

While the missiles splashed harmlessly into the Pacific there was
also a simultaneous attack launched against U.S. and South Korean
websites. While attacks against U.S. websites are common, this was
remarkable in that the United States was tied to South Korea as a
co-target. The methodology of the attack was also interesting. An old
piece of malware called MyDoom was modified and spread across the
Internet. According to South Korea's Internet and Security Agency it

was hosted on a software update server. In other words, it did not attack a new vulnerability. Analysis of the code reveals that it was written on July 3. It apparently infected 210,000 unpatched Windows desktops in less than a day and proceeded to launch denial of service attacks using Ping and GET floods. While the total bandwidth of attacks was reported to exceed 20 gigs of traffic, each target only saw, on average, 39 mbps of traffic (according to Arbor Networks ASERT). The United States reported that several of the targets including www.FTC.com (Federal Trade Commission, responsible for prosecuting spammers and spyware distributors), www.faa.com (Federal Aviation Administration), and Whitehouse.gov were effectively shut down by the attacks. Several of the targeted sites survived unharmed, including Amazon.com, which is not surprising since Amazon operates arguably the largest and most robust e-commerce site in the world. These attacks have helped to highlight the lack of preparedness on the part of South Korean banks and government sites as well as those of several branches of the U.S. government. The attacks also were the first to receive such widespread recognition in the media. Cyberwar and cyber attacks reached a new level of public awareness.

Attribution is one of the murkiest enigmas facing cyber defenders. Without knowing who is behind these attacks how can South Korea and the United States respond appropriately? Did some North Korean cyber-ops team launch these attacks as part of its continuing saber rattling? Were they attempting to demonstrate their technological prowess? If so, should the attacked countries respond either diplomatically, economically, or militarily? If the United States in particular truly cannot determine who was behind these attacks what does that say about the United States' own cyber and traditional espionage capability? Can someone launch an attack against the U.S. government and be completely hidden from discovery by the CIA, FBI, and NSA?

Let us look at possible attributions:

1. A completely uninterested cyber hacker who is motivated by the prospect of having a little fun by demonstrating his coding prowess and getting the world in a tizzy over a cyber kerfuffle.
2. China, which could be escalating from cyber espionage to cyber attack by experimenting with capabilities it has been developing. Why not let a team code up some malware and launch it as a demonstration? Make sure there is no trace leading back to China.

The U.S. and South Korea are taken down a notch in the eyes of the world and in the meantime they learn something about the effectiveness of this type of attack and its political ramifications.

3. Russia, which could use these attacks as a demonstration of Western weakness. Everyone is talking about cyber-offensive capability lately. How are nation-states to gain any experience with cyber offense if they don't get to try it out?

4. The Russian Business Network or other cyber criminal group taking advantage of the world situation to make the United States look helpless; and, incidentally, take a shot at the FTC, which is the most active branch in the U.S. government fighting the types of spam and adware that the RBN likes to use.

5. A vendor of cyber defense products that wants to generate demand for its business. Certainly Ahn Labs, a South Korean AV vendor, has been vocal about the ramifications of these attacks.

6. Islamic extremists also exploring the world of cyber attacks.

7. A student experiment run amok. Why not a modern-day Robert Morris scenario?

8. A group within the South Korean or the U.S. government launched the attacks to build their own case for improved investment in cyber warfare capabilities. (You have to include the conspiracy theory of course.)

Because of the lack of direct evidence of the source of the attacks, most analysts have erred on the conservative side and favor the first scenario above: independent hackers. Yet, if a disinterested hacker pulled this off, the fact remains that any of the other possible candidates, who do indeed exist, could observe and learn from these attacks. In other words, regardless of who orchestrated the Korean cyber attacks of July 2009, all potential adversaries learned from them. The world's militaries are paying more attention to this series of events than the victims apparently are.

So regardless of attribution we have learned:

1. It is possible to launch an effective simultaneous attack against multiple sites without being caught. In other words, while the value in political gain, destruction of enemy assets, or loss of face by an enemy is minuscule, the expense is even closer to zero; that is, the return on investment is very large.

2. It is fairly easy for anyone with a little technical know-how to execute such an attack.
3. Many high profile, albeit informational, sites are relatively easy to knock off the "Net," at least temporarily.

While complete attribution to North Korea has not been established, South Korea appears pretty convinced. Korean news sites report that in October 2009 Won Sei-hoon, chief of the South's National Intelligence Service said that the North's Ministry of Posts and Telecommunications was the culprit behind the distributed denial of service attack.

Every use of cyber attacks around the globe has new elements and different motivations. It is not possible to tie them into either a cohesive theory of modern warfare or a common set of tools and methodologies. That said, the numerous examples from so many sources paint a picture. And from that picture we can be confident that all future conflicts, be they armed, diplomatic, or just the waging of publicity campaigns, will be accompanied by cyber conflict.

DDOS DEFENSE

Denial of service is the aim of many cyber attacks: restricting access to or destroying an information asset. In this chapter we introduce Barrett Lyon, reluctant cyber warrior, as he develops DDoS defense techniques—techniques that have since been used by Estonia and are the basis for modern cyber defense.

> *To throw by strategic movements the mass of an army, successively, upon the decisive points of a theater of war, and also upon the communications of the enemy as much as possible without compromising one's own.*
>
> —Jomini's first maxim

When people first encounter Barrett Lyon it takes them only minutes to realize that he is extraordinarily intelligent. When he speaks publicly or is interviewed he begins by declaring his age because that seems to be the first thing questioners want to know, thanks to his boyish demeanor. A conversation with Barrett invariably ranges well beyond the topic at hand. His curiosity and his constant exploration of ideas led him down branching paths, but his story meanders through the development of the Internet, the infrastructure that supports it, and the nefarious elements that exploit it.

During the height of the dot com boom, the lingerie brand Victoria's Secret announced a bold initiative to broadcast video of their annual fashion show over the Internet. As a publicity stunt the event was successful. It was also a demonstration of an inherent weakness of the Internet and the architectures employed to serve up data. So many people attempted to view the Victoria's Secret models strut down the runway that the servers failed. When the crowd of viewers, using web browsers to access the video stream, caused the site to fail, they inadvertently created what is known as a Distributed Denial of Service (DDoS).

There are many ways to accomplish denial of service. The Victoria's Secret case could be considered friendly fire. Most other attacks are more malicious. Cyber activists use DDoS to shut down the servers and networks of political, religious, and corporate organizations. Cyber criminals attempt to extort cash payments from their targets with the threat of shutting down the victim's business. Small businesses have been known to hire botnets, collections of compromised computers, to shut down a competitor. Nations in conflict use crowd-sourced denial of service attacks to shut off access to critical websites in a show of force, but also to silence a vocal critic in conjunction with an invasion.

Denial of service attacks are the strongest weapon available for cyber aggression. Countering them is very expensive and could theoretically be impossible. Yet, there are measures that organizations can take to improve their defensive posture.

Let us look at the defining moments in the development of DDoS as a weapon.

In 2003 Barrett Lyon was 25 years old. His work at an IT development company presented him with an interesting task. One of their clients was being harassed by hackers in Eastern Europe. The client, Don Best Sports, was in the business of gathering and disseminating sports information. They provided the up-to-the-minute data used by Las Vegas casinos in their bookmaking operations, where gamblers place bets on game scores and even detailed performance of individual athletes. Having reliable Internet access was critical to them. Agents in the field would report every detail of even amateur sports events. Every pitch, every play would be reported by an army of sports data specialists. These results would be displayed on big boards within the casinos, where gamblers could bet on any aspect of the games.

Don Best Sports first became aware that they had a problem when they received a threatening e-mail, written convincingly in broken English, informing them that hackers had broken into their systems and encrypted their database of sports information, demanding that they pay thousands to obtain the key to decrypt the data. At this point Barrett got involved. Luckily his client was following standard practice of backing up their data and had no problem at all just restoring the back-up. But Barrett predicted that the hackers would escalate their efforts to the next level: a denial of service attack. They would use a network of computers they controlled, a botnet, to send millions of requests to their target to effectively deny anyone else's ability to access sports information. The disruption to their business could spell disaster.

Barrett helped his client quickly bolster their defensive posture. The key was to have robust web servers, gateway devices that could filter attacks, and lots and lots of available bandwidth. Within days the hackers did, indeed, attempt a denial of service attack and, thanks to Barrett's new architecture, the attack was thwarted.

Barrett was elevated to hero status overnight, and word quickly spread to the murky world of online gambling, where his services became highly sought.

Before continuing the story of Barrett Lyon and the development of effective DDoS defenses, let's take a moment for an exploration of just why DDoS is such an effective weapon.

The earliest denial of service attack was a ping flood. Anyone with a fast computer running Unix could execute a simple command that would generate ping packets, small one-way communications used by network monitoring products to check to see if a host is still responding, to completely tie up the resources of the target computer or even completely clog its network connection. At one point some servers were even vulnerable to a single packet that was constructed to make them crash. This was dubbed "The Ping of Death." Ping floods are simple to defend against. A single rule in a router or firewall between the attacker and the target can block all pings.

There are, however, some packets that cannot be simply blocked at the firewall. Packets associated with the normal operation of the attacked website (or other type of server) have to be let through. In the case of a website there is the TCP (Transmission Control Protocol) packet that initiates a connection between a browser and a web server, the SYN packet. When a web server receives a SYN packet it responds in kind, thus beginning a three-way handshake that most Internet connections start with. When it receives a third packet it can start delivering the web page or whatever has been requested. An attacker simply sends millions of SYN packets, which tie up the web server to the point where it cannot accept any more connections. Today most firewalls are capable of intercepting SYN requests. While effective defenses have been developed for blocking SYN floods, it still means deploying special equipment in the network path. Another type of attack, the GET flood, mimics thousands of web browsers requesting pages. This type of attack makes the web server work at maximum capacity serving up its pages and effectively prevents legitimate traffic from getting through.

Flood attacks using SYN and GET can be blocked if the source is known. Once again, just block all traffic from a specific IP address.

It did not take long for hackers to develop techniques for distributing their attacks among hundreds, thousands, and potentially millions of attacking hosts. This made the task of identifying and blocking the sources almost impossible. These are the most effective attack techniques known, and can be very expensive to counter. The winner is usually the one with the most available bandwidth.

There are two ways to create an army of attacking hosts. Hackers have been "recruiting" hosts by spreading malware that surreptitiously infects a computer and enlists it in a network that can be controlled from a central point and commanded to launch an attack against a target at the whim of the owner of the army of what are called "bots." These "bot armies" are available for hire and have been used to threaten and launch attacks against whitehouse.gov and other public entities. The other way to orchestrate a distributed denial of service attack is via crowd sourcing, which we discuss in another chapter.

Barrett Lyon, after demonstrating that there are effective countermeasures to DDoS, began to get requests from a very specific niche industry: online gaming sites. In 2003 there was some question about the legality of gambling online. Enough ambiguity existed that millions of U.S. citizens participated in poker, slot machines, craps, and sports betting online. There were dozens of companies providing such services, most of them hosted offshore in the Caribbean or in Costa Rica. These were very lucrative businesses. One small operation consisting of tele-operators and a closet of servers in an office in Costa Rica claimed to do $2 billion in annual revenue. At that level of turnover it is easy to understand why they were prime targets for extortion threats that targeted their online presence. Being down for even a day meant millions in lost gaming revenue.

The biggest day of the year for sports betting sites that serve the United States is Super Bowl Sunday. Leading up to Super Bowl XXXVIII in 2004, the gaming sites began to receive extortion e-mails from Eastern Europe. The letters said in effect: pay us $30,000 via Western Union by some date or we will take you off-line. The owners of the gaming sites began to call on Barrett Lyon to replicate the defenses he had created for the closely affiliated sports information operation.

It was then that Barrett had his big idea. Why ask all of these small website operators to invest in the infrastructure to counter a denial of service attack when he could make that investment once and provide a secure hosting service to all comers? But where to get financing? From one of those online gaming sites of course!

Thus Barrett embarked on a wild entrepreneurial adventure in partnership with a Costa Rican gambling operation. The new company was named Prolexic Technologies. Within a year Prolexic hosted 80 percent of the online gaming websites in the world and succeeded in putting a stop to the nascent extortion racket emanating from Eastern Europe. His efforts included working with international law enforcement to track down, prosecute, and send to prison in Siberia one of the kingpins of extortion, a young man known by his screen name, Ivan.

The architecture designed by Barrett and his team of network security whizzes used three primary elements to defend against DDoS; elements that are worth studying.

First, Prolexic would proxy a customer's web servers in their own data centers placed strategically around the world. A proxy is just a server that mimics the original site. A request for a web page would go to the Prolexic server, which would in turn retrieve the relevant web page from the original server in Costa Rica and serve it back to the requestor. By positioning a proxy server in between all transactions Prolexic could apply various defenses. These included finely tuned operating systems that would not be vulnerable to common exploits found in off-the-shelf operating systems. Barrett called on the expertise of one of the world's top BSD developers based in Hawaii. BSD is an open source version of UNIX. The community of BSD developers has focused on creating as secure an operating system as possible. Prolexic customized BSD by removing all the components not needed by a web server. Then they enhanced its ability to thwart the type of resource re-strictions (memory, open ports, etc.) that usually caused servers to fail when they received too many connections. They also developed load-balancing technology so that an attack of millions of requests could be served across multiple servers.

The next investment Prolexic made was in off-the-shelf network gear from the top providers of denial of service defense products. These devices could detect attacks, send alerts, and throttle attack packets. The cost for such devices can exceed $100K and the special security knowledge to run them is not readily available to a typical organiza-tion. Prolexic could make that investment because they were protecting multiple paying clients.

The final component of Prolexic's defense was bandwidth. The typi-cal heavily trafficked website uses 10–20 megabits per second of band-width. Through its relationships with major backbone Internet provid-ers Prolexic could use up to 18 gigabits per second of bandwidth, an unprecedented amount. Most Internet services see the largest amount of bandwidth for outward-bound traffic. YouTube, Google's video host-ing service, has to supply terabits of data to its consumers of stream-ing video. So negotiating contracts with carriers for large amounts of incoming traffic is relatively easy and inexpensive. The largest attack Prolexic experienced was 11 gigs of traffic. According to Verisign, an Internet company that has its own DDoS defense service, DDoS attacks can exceed 60 gigs of traffic today.

These measures: hardened, load-balanced servers; defensive devices, and massive amounts of available bandwidth are the core of DDoS defense.

There is an Achilles' heel of web infrastructure that attackers have recognized and attacked: the Domain Name Service (DNS). The In-ternet is based on protocols that use source and destination addresses to route traffic. When a web address, a URL, is entered into a web browser, there has to be some way to translate www.threatchaos.com to 69.65.42.159, its IP address, before packets can be exchanged and a visitor can see a web page. The DNS is a layer of servers all over the world that provide that function. It is a simple protocol, but execut-ing it is becoming more complicated as more and more demands are being put on it.

There are multiple tiers to the DNS. The Top Level Domains (TLD) are .com, .net, .gov, .edu, and the many country codes such as .ee for

Estonia, .ge for Georgia, .ru for Russia, and .uk for the United Kingdom. Each of these top level domains is supported by different organizations. When you type www.threatchaos.com in to the URL window of your browser you generate a request to the .com TLD server (hosted by Verisign in over 400 data centers around the world.) That server replies with the IP address of the name server that is responsible for keeping track of all of the IP addresses associated with the domain Threatchaos.com. Your browser quickly checks with that server (NS1 .MEDIALAYER at 72.249.28.154) which promptly directs you to www .threatchaos.com.

While an owner of a website could take measures to protect his server he may not own the DNS server that provides the critical function of pointing at the website. In other words, an attacker could target the DNS server and effectively take down the website. The problem is compounded because a DNS server often provides name service for hundreds, even thousands, of separate domains.

This introduces the concept of collateral damage. You may not know what other domains are served by the DNS machine that you rely on. It could be a political site that attracts the ire of hacktivists. An attack on the political site could take your own site down. So one additional measure to countering DDoS is to own your own separate DNS server and protect it with similar defenses: hardened, load-balanced servers; specialized network gear; and lots of bandwidth.

A few months after Barrett parted ways with the management of Prolexic, his reputation as the master of DDoS defense brought him into another situation. A popular e-commerce site headquartered in the San Francisco Bay Area had grown rapidly by hosting easy-to-set-up storefronts for its customers. These web-based storefronts would provide hats, mugs, and t-shirts to consumers imprinted with any image, message, or artwork the owner of each storefront desired. One entrepreneur chose to sell t-shirts with images of the Islamic prophet Mohammed. These were the same cartoons that had been published in a Danish newspaper *Jyllands-Postenin*. Fundamentalist Islam forbids the creation of any sort of image of people, let alone of the Prophet. When *Jyllands-Postenin* printed those cartoons there were violent protests in many cities around the world that led to hundreds of deaths. In the weeks leading up to Christmas 2006 the e-commerce company received a threatening e-mail claiming to come from Islamic Jihad, a known terrorist organization. The e-mail demanded that the merchandise be removed. The e-commerce site opted to ignore the threats. When a massive denial of service attack was directed at them (a graph created automatically by the Netcraft.com service verifies the outage), they tracked down Barrett and begged him to help. Barrett was in the middle of launching a new venture, Bitgravity, a content delivery network (CDN), so he declined their offers. Until, that is, they told him to name a price. Consider the importance of being available to customers during the Christmas buying season to a venture-backed web company. A prolonged outage could put them out of business. Barrett acquiesced and collected a fee that helped him fund the first year's development of his next venture. Needless to say he had them back online within hours, using the techniques he pioneered at Prolexic. He spent several days looking at the source of the attack and verified that over 1,000 bots had been involved and were controlled from a server in the Middle East, and the domain name had been hijacked, also from the Middle East. This was significant evidence that an Islamic terrorist group had become familiar with the techniques of DDoS.

BORDER GATEWAY PROTOCOL:
THE NAKED UNDERBELLY OF THE INTERNET

The Internet is a marvel of self-organization with many components that work seamlessly on top of each other. Web servers, layers of protocols, social networks, and routing infrastructure all work together to provide a communication, business, and social platform that is fueling change in society and the world of commerce. But those underlying components were designed and deployed before today's threats were apparent.

There is a weak link in the way the Internet is architected. It is the underlying routing protocol. This weak link is well known by aggressors, but has not been exploited in an overt malicious act. Yet.

YouTube is a popular video-sharing site that Google acquired from its founders in October 2006. Over 100 million people visit YouTube monthly to watch six billion downloaded videos.

On February 24, 2008, an engineer at an ISP in Pakistan removed YouTube from the Internet. He did this in response to a government decree. His intention was to follow the letter of the law and block access to YouTube from within Pakistan. There are several ways this could have been accomplished but here is the method he chose.

Packets on the Internet flow through routers that are responsible for forwarding them on to the next router on the best path to their destination. These routers maintain a list of routes based on blocks of IP addresses. When a packet is received the router reads its intended destination, looks it up in a big table and forwards it on to the next router. Where does that router get that big table? From other routers, of course. The protocol used to transmit those route tables is Border Gateway Protocol (BGP). An ISP will have a huge block of IP addresses assigned to them by ARIN (American Registry for Internet Numbers). But they do not want to be bothered with updating their routers every time a customer makes a change to the way they use the IP addresses assigned to them, so the ISP gives their biggest customers the ability to update the routing tables on their own. The customer, say Google, then updates their own routers, which use BGP to announce which IP addresses it controls to the rest of the routers on the Internet. A router on the other side of the world would see that ATT owns the big block of addresses that they assigned to Google but would treat Google's own announcement of the IP address range that YouTube resides at as the authoritative source because it is the more granular route announcement.

What happens if an even smaller route announcement is published via BGP? That is exactly what happened in Pakistan. The engineer at PIENet loaded a new route into his router that said the small block of addresses that contained the IP address of www.youtube.com were controlled by him. The result was almost instantaneous. His upstream provider in Hong Kong picked up the new route and broadcast it to the world. Most routers treated those routes as authoritative because they were more granular than those announced by Google. Every request to watch a YouTube video was routed from anywhere in the world to a small ISP in Pakistan. YouTube was effectively removed from the Internet. Those requests were so numerous that they flooded Pakistan's Internet knocking Pakistan off the Internet as well.

Barrett Lyon was serendipitously at the center of this event as well. After founding Prolexic and building it into a success, Barrett launched a new venture. BitGravity is a content delivery network (CDN) that Barrett created from scratch. As the Internet has begun to carry more and more video, the strain put on delivery mechanisms has grown. Live streaming of a single event like Victoria's Secret's runway show was a first. Now conferences, video chat, online "Internet TV" shows, and services like YouTube and Hulu put even greater demands on infrastructure. Comedy Central, Revision3, CollegeHumor, and uncountable pornography sites rely on CDNs to deliver their content. These services are willing to pay for reliable delivery of their programming. Barrett built BitGravity to serve that market. BitGravity is backed, in part, by the largest backbone bandwidth provider in the world, TaTa Communications, based in India. This gives BitGravity access to that bandwidth. Barrett's activity also puts him at the hub of a community of people who manage Internet traffic.

It is not surprising that when YouTube was routed to Pakistan, Barrett was on a private chat channel with those operators. A few quick checks of the routing tables and they had figured out exactly what had happened. Barrett found himself calling engineers at PCCW in Hong Kong and telling them how to filter the route announcements coming from Pakistan. Thanks to Barrett Lyon the YouTube outage was repaired by the end of that fateful Sunday.

The Pakistan–YouTube incident of 2008 demonstrated just how effective spurious BGP route announcements could be as a cyber weapon. While not malicious, the effects were completely effective in denying access to YouTube.

Preventing malicious abuse of BGP is a concern of the Internet community as a whole and is being addressed, but in the meantime it is critical that an organization's upstream Internet provider follow best practices by installing strict controls over which routers and networks they will accept BGP route announcements from. If you control your own block of IP addresses and do your own route announcements, one defensive measure would be to be ready to announce very small blocks of addresses if a YouTube-like attack occurs. Another defense could be to move your site to a completely different block of IP addresses, hosted by another ISP, that the attacker has not tampered with.

Denial of service is often the intent of Internet attacks. New methods of accomplishing a denial of service are being invented every day. DNS attacks, crowd sourcing, spurious BGP route announcements, and botnets are today's weapons of choice. Future methodologies will become apparent as attackers push the envelope. Luckily, Barrett Lyon and legions of equally skilled engineers are watching over the Internet; call them Internet Guardian Angels.

Relying on ad hoc responses may actually be the appropriate way to respond to the current cyber threat environment. Just as markets do a better job of regulating good and bad business practices in rapidly evolving economies, the self-interested protection of the security community may be the best response to the scourge of Internet pestilence. Viruses, worms, spam, spyware, and botnets have all changed the Internet and the way organizations use it. In the next chapter we address the rise of state involvement and response to cyber threats.

CROWD SOURCING
CYBER ATTACKS

In this chapter, we address the rise of crowd sourced cyber attacks: using large numbers of independent recruits to target websites and critical infrastructure for destruction or damage. The advantage of an effective cyber weapon that is almost impossible to attribute to a particular aggressor makes crowd sourcing ideal for political manipulation concurrent with physical attacks. We also examine the use of crowd sourcing to sway public opinion in China.

> *You blocks, you stones, you worse than senseless things!*
>
> —Marullus

The power of thousands of individuals acting in concert has become a weapon of war. While politicians, revolutionaries, and totalitarian governments have long known the effectiveness of sending crowds of protesters to the streets to parade in front of television cameras, the new trend is to mobilize forces over the Internet to engage in the equivalent of mass online protests. In some cases the results can be humorous. In others, not.

Superiority in numbers has long been the decisive factor in winning battles. Tactics evolve with changing technologies. Tragically, those tactics usually lag the introduction of the technology. Concentration of forces in the field using swords and spears reigned from the time of the battles of the Peloponnesian wars all the way to the introduction of musketry in the 1700s, when large armies of conscripted soldiers were outfitted with muzzle loaders and sent in human waves against each other or against entrenched forces. Napoleon perfected the combination of mass attacks of infantry with artillery bombardments and flanking cavalry. If the enemy massed in a square formation to counter the cavalry the artillery would destroy it. If they spread out in a long front to counter the infantry they would be swept up by the cavalry attacking from the side. Yet lessons learned from Napoleon were misinterpreted by theorists such as Jomini and Clausewitz, members of his staff, and led to the misapplication of human wave attacks during World War I. The Battle of the Somme saw over 600,000 casualties on the Allied side and even more on the German side as three months of successive human waves were launched across fields strung with barbed wire, swept by machine guns, and constantly bombarded by artillery.

The human wave attack is still resorted to today when one side has large numbers of untrained poorly armed soldiers who are sent against smaller forces of highly trained, well-armed defenders. The results are usually disastrous. During the Iran-Iraq war, Iran sent massed troops ranging in age from nine to 50 years old across minefields while under constant fire to clear the way for tanks and mechanized infantry. The total casualties in this war of attrition that eventually beat back Iraq were over 160,000 people.

The Information Age that we have entered introduces new technology at a rate that is orders of magnitude faster than ever before. Modern wars are dependent on good information-gathering from satellite reconnaissance, espionage, communication from the field, and reliable command and control. Any tool, mechanism, or weapon that can disrupt the free flow of, or access to, information can and will be used in future conflicts.

Much of the U.S. Comprehensive Cyber Security Initiative is focused on information sharing. Of the twelve projects incorporated in the document, four are devoted to sharing of information between government and the private sector, various research labs, the Computer Emergency Response Teams, and with service providers. Ironically, investing in better information sharing between the thousands of units of government only makes information and communication a more valuable target and therefore more likely to be attacked. The cyber battles in evidence today target lines of communication, intelligence gathering, and critical infrastructure. Crowd sourcing is a new phenomenon. Wikipedia, itself a crowd sourced online repository of knowledge, has a definition:

> Crowd sourcing is a neologism for the act of taking a task traditionally performed by an employee or contractor, and outsourcing it to an undefined, generally large group of people, in the form of an open call. For example, the public may be invited to develop a new technology, carry out a design task, refine or carry out the steps of an algorithm or help capture, systematize or analyze large amounts of data.[1]

During the U.S. presidential elections of 2008 any online poll was quickly inundated with votes derived from a call to arms by the followers of one candidate or the other, with Ron Paul, the small-government libertarian, usually winning out because of his appeal to the tech-savvy.

Crowd sourced attacks can have amusing consequences. Grassroots campaigns can spring up quickly to address a cause or an online vote in order to sway public opinion. In an attempt to garner sympathy for its cause, Greenpeace created a poll to choose a name for a whale. A call to the members of reddit, the popular social bookmarking site, was put out. It read:

> Greenpeace are having a vote to name a whale they have "adopted." All the options are the names of ancient gods of the sea. And then there's "Mister Splashy Pants." Please vote "Mister Splashy Pants."

Greenpeace demonstrated extremely good humor in accepting the results of over 100,000 votes for "Mr. Splashy Pants," the humpback whale they were tracking via satellite.

Vladimir Vladimirovich Putin, prime minister of Russia, has learned to use crowd sourcing to orchestrate massive denial of service attacks capable of shutting off an entire country's ability to access the Internet. Included in his growing list of successful attacks are Estonia 2007, Lithuania 2007, Ukraine 2007, Georgia 2008, and Krgyzstan 2009. Putin commands a youth group called the Nashi, which meet every summer for fresh air, exercise, and indoctrination. When it comes time to spread a little trouble, an operative posts instructions for downloading tools for launching denial of service attacks along with a list of targets. Nashi, and anyone similarly motivated, then downloads the tools and kicks off the targeted attacks; DDoS by crowd sourcing. The beauty is that this technique provides a shield of plausible deniability: "This was not Russia it was a bunch of patriots that were angry at fascists/Estonia (etc.)."

Security researchers follow crowd sourced attacks as they occur, but few have attempted to explain the development over time. Here is one way of looking at the rise of crowd sourced attacks as a tool of cyberwar by Russia. The successful mass demonstrations, sit-ins, and civil protests of the Ukrainian Orange Revolution in the fall of 2004 resulted in the peaceful election of a democratic president in January of 2005. The Orange Revolution was an example of traditional, noncyber, crowd sourcing that led to regime change. It created consternation within Russia, particularly with then president Putin. Russia's reaction was to create a youth movement of its own, hoping to enlist the power of crowds to ward off any similar democratic revolt in Moscow. The formation of the Nashi was announced three months later, and the first mass meeting was held April 15, 2005. A loose translation of what "Nashi" stands for is "Youth Democratic Anti-Fascist Movement Ours!" The nationalist group, ironically, is reminiscent of Hitler's brown-shirted, fascist, Nazi Youth. They have a red flag with a white X as an emblem, and their stated tactics are to engage in street fighting to counter the imagined threat from "skin heads." Its 120,000 members are called out in force to demonstrate in pro-Putin rallies, and in effect create an environment of fear that is not conducive to political dissent.

The Nashi, made up of young people, is well suited to crowd sourced attacks. They share a political mind and have the computer skills to join a call for an attack. Each member can devise their own techniques and use the tools to which they have access. That is the power of crowd sourcing after all. It uses the combined resources of many individuals to achieve its purpose. When that purpose is malicious, the results are devastating.

As we shall see in the following chapters, crowd sourced DDoS was used effectively against several former Soviet states.

The mounting evidence that nation-states are engaging in cyber attacks against each other's data, communications, and infrastructure is harder to depict as a threat to the typical IT department. A hospital, insurance firm, or university may claim that they are not targets of espionage and that cyber warfare is something that only the Defense

Department should be concerned with. They would be wrong on the espionage side, as evidenced by China's apparent infinite appetite for industrial and research data. But they would also be wrong about cyber warfare. There is a real and present danger that these skirmishes could boil over into network outages that impact everyone.

During the January 2009 military action in Gaza, attacks against Israeli and American websites became another example of a crowd sourced cyber attack. Dozens of attackers systematically defaced over 800 websites with pro-Hamas messages, many of them depicting gruesome images of dead babies and wounded civilians. Among the sites attacked were Israeli news sites, government servers, and even hospitals that were treating Palestinian casualties of the Gaza war. Crowd sourced attacks were not limited to the Hamas side. At least one Israeli site posted instructions for attacking Hamas websites.

Every age brings its new methods of warfare. The Romans perfected field combat with foot soldiers. Napoleon developed modern staffing for command and control, combined with the science of logistics for resupply, and the use of cannon batteries in conjunction with tactically deployed corps of infantry and cavalry. World War I saw the introduction of poison gas and mechanized armies. World War II introduced aviation, missiles, and rockets to the mix. The world has been suspended in an uneasy equilibrium since the threat of nuclear holocaust was introduced at the start of the Cold War. Vietnam was the most tragic example of the use of guerrilla warfare to vanquish the techniques and technology of World War II–era armies. The so-called terror war is seeing the rise of cells, suicide bombers, and IED's (improvised explosive devices, such as the roadside bombs used in Iraq and Afghanistan against U.S. troops) as effective weapons. While defacing websites and disabling government communication vehicles such as the Ministry of Foreign Affairs site of the Georgian government (www .mfa.gov.ge) have not yet been recognized as warfare, it is apparent that networks, which have had an immeasurably positive impact on communication, commerce, and social interaction, are also vulnerable to attacks. Attacks on and across networks are poised to become the defining innovation of twenty-first-century warfare.

The motivation for using a disbursed and large group of nonprofessionals in a cyber attack is both political and technical. Political advantage arises from the plausible deniability. China still maintains the fiction that attacks against the Pentagon, France, Germany, India,

Australia, and New Zealand that emanated from within its borders are the acts of unaffiliated young hackers. Even now Russia does not accept responsibility for attacks against Estonia, Lithuania, Ukraine, or Georgia, although a Nashi youth has claimed credit for the Estonian attacks. Russia, perhaps the most accomplished country at manipulating world opinion, continues to deny all responsibility for its well-orchestrated attacks that have not only brought down the immediate targets, such as websites of government agencies, but have effectively brought Internet traffic to a halt in the targeted regions.

TWITTER

Twitter is a social networking phenomenon that has blossomed into a tool for organizing popular protest. First created to allow people to use a free service to broadcast text messages to multiple recipients, it has morphed into a communication tool used by over thirty million people. Users log on to their Twitter page and post whatever is on their mind. That seemingly simplistic concept has had a remarkable impact on messaging, "social bookmarking," and the spread of world news. The first news and even images and videos of earthquakes, celebrity deaths, and sporting results are broadcast as they happen. Twitter users pick up and spread information as they see it. An image, captured on a cell phone, of passengers standing on the wings of ditched flight #1549 in the Hudson River was famously posted to Twitter by user jkrums, who was on a ferry that raced to the scene.

One mechanism for spreading news is to Re-Tweet (RT) messages of interest. The other mechanism is the hash tag. By appending a # (hash mark) to a key word everyone can follow a topic of conversation using the Twitter search feature. In recent months Twitter has enhanced their service by adding a list of trending topics to the Twitter page of each user so that they can see the most talked about or Re-Tweeted topics. This serves to exacerbate or enhance the spread of breaking news.

Twitter Has Become a Tool of Political Change and Even Crowd Sourced Cyber Attacks

Moldova is a small country snuggled up against the Carpathian Mountains in Eastern Europe. Like many ex-Soviet satellite states it is still struggling with the demise of Communism and has old-guard Communists seeking to stay in power under the guise of democracy. An election in April 2009 led to protests in the streets over a Communist win. What was new was the widespread use of Twitter. Organizers would broadcast their plans via Twitter, which they could access via the web or their cell phones. Blogs of political dissidents were linked to and spread via Twitter. One blogger, Natalia Morar, was temporarily put under house arrest for her activities. The hash tag #pman (acronym for Piata Marii Adunari Nationale), the name of a square where protests were held, was used to track all of the Tweets of the activists. Even after new elections were held the Communists remained in power, but more elections are planned.

In Moldova, Twitter's role was one of communication and spreading the word of events that otherwise were not covered by traditional media. Shortly thereafter Twitter played a much larger role in world events.

Twitter Enlists the Crowd to Disable
Iranian Government Sites

On Friday, June 12, 2009, Iran held a general election for president. Within hours of the polls' closing the incumbent, President Mahmoud Ahmadinejad was announced as the clear winner with a 64 percent majority of the popular vote. The population of Iran erupted in outrage over the results, which they believed were suspect. Hundreds of thousands of people flooded into the streets and lined rooftops shouting "Allahu Akbar." The Iranian government deployed their organized supporters, the Basij militia, who attacked student dormitories and terrorized the populace with beatings, rock throwing, and shootings. Over the ensuing weekend Twitter erupted in a flood of messages first generated by Iranians on the streets of Tehran, then picked up and Re-Tweeted by thousands of online sympathizers. People began to change their Twitter avatars to a green background, representing the green flags and banners of the opposition supporters of Mir-Hossein Mousavi to show their solidarity with the protesters and an honest democratic process. The hash tags #iranelections and #iran soared to the top of the "trending topics" and at one point accounted for 2.5 percent of all Tweets posted.

By the following Monday, June 15, the first use of Twitter as a tool for fomenting cyber attacks appeared. In a remarkably fast evolution,

Twitter was exploited to enlist thousands of people in targeted cyber attacks.

The first phase of Twitter-induced DDoS reflected the most common practice in previous crowd sourced attacks. Tweets appeared that provided links to instructions for downloading common hacking tools that would execute Ping and Get floods. The download sites included instructions for targeting a list of Iranian government websites including www.leader.ir and www.president.ir. The messages were Re-Tweeted by many, and the instructions followed by those who wanted to contribute in some way to the protest led to Iranian government websites being disabled.

But downloading software is complicated, and the average Twitter user is going to be wary of installing hacking tools that could very well contain malicious code. So the next phase, introduced within 24 hours, made it simpler. Tweets were posted and spread that linked to pages that had specially formulated hyperlinks that used a service provided by pagereload.com. Clicking on those links would launch a separate tab in one's browser that would continuously refresh the targeted web page. One such list of links was even harbored on a GoogleDocs page, a collaborative word processing tool.

By the third day this technique had evolved to its simplest form. Protest supporters would just Tweet the pagereload.com URLs directly. Click on the link provided and your browser would launch an attack. A final tool that was created was a page with 15 separate frames. Each frame would continuously reload a separate target web page.

While these tactics were effective in the short term, most of the sites targeted by these Twitter-enhanced crowd sourced attacks were only disabled for brief periods. The effectiveness of this type of crowd sourcing is analogous to trying to get a crowd at a sporting event to participate in a chant. A few rabble rousers in the crowd can ignite a coordinated chant, but the participants soon weary or are distracted by the action on the field. Participants in the Twitter-spawned attacks would get tired of having their browser reloading all those pages and their one Internet connection clogged with the traffic. So the instigators needed to constantly renew their message to keep up the attack.

The long-term impact of the Iran cyber protests may be the education that thousands of people received thanks to a few hacktivists. The population of people who understand the use of DDoS as a tool of protest has grown much larger. Future political and world events may incite new protests that will be directed by social media such as Twitter.

Another lesson learned from the Iran protest on Twitter is the use of social media for counter-psychological operations. See the later discussion on cyber psyops, misdirection, and message integrity.

THOUGHT CONTROL VIA CROWD SOURCING

Targeted attacks are just one use for crowd sourcing in the ongoing battle between nations, ideologies, and politicians. The Chinese government is using crowd sourcing to influence public opinion, a method of thought control, or psyops.

But first, some history: bloggers have become the modern-day political dissidents. They leverage the Internet to become as powerful as an underground newspaper. They are like the pamphleteers who helped catalyze the American Revolution. Totalitarian countries, especially China, are waging a war against the sometimes elusive revolutionary bloggers who criticize their policies and actions.

On New Year's Eve 2004, Microsoft's MSN blogging service took down the controversial blog of Zhao Jing, a Beijing journalist who called for a walkout of journalists. This was at the request of the Chinese government.

In January 2005, China's ruling Communist Party demonstrated their ability to censor news items when the former leader and prodemocracy reformer Zhao Ziyang died. They forbade Chinese news organizations from reporting his death, other than a simple statement that he had died, and blocked access to sites that reported the death.

Also in 2005, a 37-year-old Chinese journalist, Shi Tao, who worked for *Contemporary Business News* in Hunan Province, sent an e-mail containing text from a Chinese Communist Party communiqué warning newspapers of the dangers of social unrest resulting from dissidents returning to Tiananmen Square on the fifteenth anniversary of the massacre. The IP address of Shi Tao's computer was handed over to the Chinese government by his e-mail provider, Yahoo. Shi Tao is now serving a ten-year prison sentence.

In January 2006 Google bowed to Chinese pressure and began censoring search results available to the people of China. Information on

Tiananmen Square, Tibet, and the passive Falun Gong movement are not available through Google searches in China.

China uses an automated search tool dubbed Night Crawler to scan content hosted within its borders and block access to IP addresses that host web pages that refer to certain key phrases such as "human rights," "Taiwan independence," "freedom," "democracy" and "demonstration."

In addition to pressuring Google, Microsoft, and Yahoo to reveal the identity of outspoken bloggers, China has stepped into the world of social networking with a vengeance. China is crowd sourcing social influence by making micro payments to an army of blog commentators. Their task is to respond to blogs and forums that question China's leadership with progovernment comments. Targeted almost exclusively at Chinese bloggers, this "50 cent army" actually sways the conversation to create a more affable opinion of Chinese actions. If Thomas Paine had been a blogger would Google have outed him to the British government? Would he have been able to stand the onslaught of public opinion as represented by a crowd of 300,000 paid commentators? Crowd sourcing is proving to be a powerful weapon in China's attempt to control public opinion. As we will see shortly, there are also groups that work to promulgate the Dalai Lama's positions and message of peace by engaging in similar activity from their positions in India just across the border of Tibet.

CNN DDOS

Crowd sourced attacks can be attributed to Chinese motivations as well. Two events occurred in April 2008 that demonstrated China's use of crowd sourcing. Dancho Danchev, a frequent blogger on the uses of botnets and DDoS attacks, analyzed the April 17–18 attacks on CNN .com, which was taken off-line for three hours. Danchev reported the two forms of attack that were used. One was a botnet directed from China to attack CNN.com; the other was a crowd sourced attack.

This botnet attack took a new turn. Participants were encouraged to allow their PCs to be infected with a Trojan, enlisting them in a bot army whose sole purpose was to direct TCP requests to a page at CNN .com. The Trojan was antiCNN.exe, specifically customized for the attack. The attacks were coordinated from anticnn.cn, a web server set up just for the project. The motivation was CNN's reporting on Tibet. Thanks to Danchev we have a very telling quote from the organizers:

> Our team of non-governmental organisations, We only private network enthusiasts. However, we have a patriotic heart, We will absolutely not permit any person to discredit our motherland under any name, We are committed to attack some spreading false information, and malicious slander, libel, support Tibet independence site.[2]

But Danchev claims a second, much more effective attack, was launched at the same time using simple scripts hosted on dozens of Chinese websites (he provides the URLs of 39 such sites). Messages were posted to over 5,000 Chinese forums exhorting "patriots" to click on links that would take them to those scripts, which would open up multiple frames in their browsers, all loading CNN.com at once.

CNN was able to thwart the attack thanks to its originating almost exclusively from China. They blocked incoming requests from Chinese IP addresses. Of course, this prevented anyone in China who wanted to see the CNN Tibet coverage from seeing it. The attacks forced CNN to be complicit in the censorship China desired.

Coincident with the attack on CNN was a separate attack on Slideshare.com, the free service that hosts slide shows and PowerPoint presentations for easy viewing. Several users had posted their presentations on China there. The level of interaction between the attackers and Slideshare is interesting to note. Slideshare reports that they received over 50 phone calls from people falsely claiming to be the owners of the presentations requesting password resets. This was a social engineering attempt to gain control of the offending accounts so that the information could be taken down. Slideshare also received irate anonymous calls demanding that the presentations be taken down. When they reviewed the content and found that it did not violate their content policies they took no action. Subsequently, Slideshare.com was taken down via DDoS attack.

In another example of collateral damage, the Sports Network was also taken over by the Chinese hackers who mistook it for CNN sports.

Technological innovation plays an important role in the history of warfare. The first generation of battles following the innovation invariably misapplies the new weapon. But, with time, warfare takes on a new face until the next innovation in technology. Crowd sourcing of web-based tasks is less than a decade old. As a weapon of conflict between nation-states the use of crowd sourcing dates from Estonia, 2007. DDoS attacks executed by thousands of independent operatives pose a threat that splashes over onto innocent bystanders. Businesses, parents and students, researchers, and individuals all become potential collateral damage from the network outages that result from crowd sourced attacks.

OH ESTONIA

The Russian attacks against Estonia ushered in the era of cyber conflict. The world has responded to the specter of loss of critical infrastructure that encompasses a whole country. We cannot identify the source, yet we also cannot deny the effects.

The ability to get to the verge without getting into the war is the necessary art. If you try to run away from it, if you are scared to go to the brink, you are lost.

—John Foster Dulles

Visitors to Tallinn, the capital of Estonia, are treated to a vision of the digital future. The city has created a Demo Center to showcase what a small country can do by leapfrogging generations of technology. It is housed in what used to be the warehouse district behind a newly constructed international airport. It contains a conference room dedicated to meetings between visiting dignitaries to Estonia and technologists from Estonia's IT industry who explain Estonia's use of digital certificates, cell phones, and electronic payments systems to make possible electronic banking, voting, tax services, and even parking via texting.

Modern Estonia is a young democracy that was released from the suffocating blanket of the Soviet Union when the giant experiment in socialism finally fell, along with the symbolic Wall in Berlin. Its president, Toomas Hendrik Ilves, was raised and educated in the United States. He speaks of malware, bots, and DDoS with a pure East Coast accent. He shoulders the concerns that any tiny nation within 120 miles of St. Petersburg would have: How do we maintain a sovereign democratic state in the shadow of a state seeking influence and hegemony over Eastern Europe, especially one that subjugated its near neighbors for decades?

Over its history, Estonia has been whipsawed by opposing forces from the West and East. It declared its independence from the Russian Empire in 1918 as Germany pushed the Russian army back at the conclusion of World War I. In the summer of 1939, before World War II started, Germany signed a nonaggression pact with the Soviet Union after agreeing to the infamous Molotov–Ribbentrop Pact and its Secret Additional Protocol that partitioned Eastern Europe into "spheres of influence." The following spring, as Hitler's mechanized army rolled through Belgium and France, forced the British Expeditionary Force into the sea, and occupied Paris, the Soviet Union blockaded Tallinn and forced the Estonian government to accept Soviet troops and bases. An invasion of 90,000 Soviet troops forced the capitulation of Estonia on June 17, 1940, and the following August, Estonia was officially, and illegally, annexed to the Soviet Union, becoming the Soviet Socialist Republic of Estonia. When Germany turned on the USSR in the summer of 1941 it pushed the Red Army out and occupied Estonia at the end of August. And as World War II drew to an end, the Soviet Empire returned to resubjugate Estonia, the third time in half a century that Estonia was under foreign rule. It was not until August of 1991 that Estonia regained its independence.

The crumbling of the Soviet Union in 1991 allowed a new Estonia to be formed. This Estonia was quickly ushered into the Information Age. Rather than invest in landline infrastructure, Estonia capitalized on the move to wireless communications. Today per capita ownership of cell phones exceeds 100 percent because many of its 1.4 million citizens own multiple digital devices for communicating. Over 80 percent bank online. Eighty percent vote online. There are 1,200 free WiFi hot spots in Tallinn. Estonians pay for parking with their cell phones by texting a code they find posted in every parking lot to a central server that keeps track of their parking time and bills them through their cell phone provider.

Estonia leads the world in e-government, using digital technology to provide information, register voters, maintain records, and support law enforcement. Each branch of government maintains its own applications and databases that are protected by standardized gateway firewalls. This "X-Road" can be accessed by law enforcement and other agencies, but every access is logged and will soon be transparent to citizens who will be able to see who looked at what records. This transparency addresses the privacy concerns that an integrated e-government could cause.

In a practice as old as the human creation of states, the Soviet Union had resettled ethnic Russians to Estonia. As Russia began to attempt to reassert itself in its ex-satellite states it leveraged local Russian-speaking populations to influence elections and attempted to get pro-Russia governments installed in many of them. (Examples: Ukraine, Kyrgyzstan, etc.) Meanwhile, in 2004 Estonia aligned itself with NATO, the collection of mutual defense treaty participants that had been established after World War II to counter the Soviet threat in Europe.

Estonia maintains a small standing army directed from a Defense Ministry housed in a three-story building in downtown Tallinn. The Estonian National Opera house across the street employs more people than are housed in the Defense Ministry. In April of 2007 Russia orchestrated a crisis that challenged Estonia's sovereignty. Estonia had set the stage for internal conflict by making fluency in Estonian a requirement for citizenship in the new democracy, a measure aimed at the ethnic Russian population settled there by the old Soviet Union. At the center of the conflict was the Bronze Soldier, a bigger than life statue of a Soviet soldier erected in central Tallinn in 1947. In an attempt to celebrate its freedom from its ties to the old regime, Estonia announced that the statue and the graves of the soldiers buried around it would be moved to a military cemetery on the outskirts of town. While attribution of who instigated the ensuing riots is hard to establish, it was a polarizing event that set ethnic Russians against ethnic Estonians. "Fascist" became the rallying cry of the pro-Russian crowds as they gathered in candlelight vigils, flower-laying ceremonies, and ultimately looting and burning of Tallinn's shopping district. Video evidence depicts the same young ethnic Russians, possibly Nashi, at each outburst, apparently engaged in rabble rousing.

The next phase of the protests took Estonia by surprise: massive denial of service attacks against Estonia's banking, telecom, and government infrastructure that commenced as soon as the Bronze Soldier was relocated. The head of security at Swedbank's Estonian subsidiary reports that over 80,000 unique IP addresses were identified as the source of the attacks, which included Get floods and Ping floods (see chapter 7 on DDoS). Fax machines and cell phones of members of Parliament were deluged with calls. Key web servers of government agencies, banks, and the office of the president succumbed to the attacks.

The cyber attacks on Estonia began Friday, April 27, 2007, and lasted several weeks. Russian-language forums carried instructions for downloading denial of service tools and identified targets at which to point those tools. Nashi activity in Moscow escalated as well, with riots outside the Estonian embassy and a crowd of forty accosting the Estonian ambassador to Russia, Marina Kaljurand, as she attended a press conference at a Moscow newspaper and later as she left the building.

On May 2, the state-owned Russian Railways halted shipments of oil and coal to Estonia, claiming they had to work on the rail line that linked the two countries.

In a move that recalls a similar visit to Tallinn in 1939 by a Soviet delegation, members of Russia's Duma flew to Tallinn on May 2 to demand the resignation of Estonia's government. They were summarily dismissed and put on a plane back to Moscow.

From Radio Free Europe:

> Estonian President Toomas Hendrik Ilves criticized Russia in comments quoted on May 2. "I turn to Russia, Estonia's neighbor, with a clear message—try to remain civilized!" AP quoted Ilves as saying in a statement. He also said it is "not customary in Europe" to "use computers belonging to public institutions for cyber-attacks against another country's public institutions," or to "demand the resignation of the democratically elected government of another sovereign country."[1]

And according to the Associated Press, Ilves also urged Estonia's Russian speakers to "learn Estonian, be successful, be happy!"

President Ilves alludes to evidence Estonia had that some of the cyber attacks originated from within the Kremlin (one of the attacking IP addresses) although subsequent investigations have yet to yield conclusive attribution to the Russian government for the attack. As stressed in chapter 7, one of the reasons crowd sourced attacks are powerful modern weapons is their "plausible deniability." The instigator can claim public outrage as the cause, not centrally led command and control.

Estonia's response and recovery from cyber attack is important to understand. It took three phases: communication, network response, and server infrastructure hardening.

The Internet itself would not have grown to the extent it has if it were not for the communication and collaboration channels that network administrators keep open. In the early days of the Internet, as each hosting and network domain was established, the owners would publicize their contact information via the domain name registry maintained by a small company called Network Solutions that was responsible for registering each new domain name and making that information available via what is called a "whois" lookup. If there were an issue with a particular route announced for IP traffic or a particular service hosted on a network attached computer, someone would look up the owner of the problem device or network and give them a call to get the issue resolved quickly.

As spammers discovered the value of e-mail addresses and used the Whois database to harvest them, the viability of that database for problem resolution disappeared. It was replaced by ad hoc lists and private groups. The North American Network Operators Group (NANOG) holds annual get-togethers where network administrators make key connections, and semiofficial Computer Emergency Response Teams (CERTs) have been established to ensure that network outages, routing issues, and cyber attacks can be responded to quickly.

In April of 2007, the technical community of Estonia found itself enlisted in an ad hoc team to counter the Russian cyber attacks. They became cyber warriors. Within an hour of the start of the DDoS attacks against Estonia's computing infrastructure, key personnel from the Defense Ministry, the major telecom providers, the banks, and the university located in Tartu were talking to each other to determine what was happening and what needed to be done.

The first step was to stop the flood of attacks from the widespread botnets. The network administrators at the carriers started to filter out all communication from outside Estonia. They essentially cut Estonia off from the Internet. This allowed online banking to continue and local information sources to be available to citizens. (In response the attackers recruited bots inside Estonia and continued the DDoS against critical servers.)

The next step was to address a fundamental problem with the way the government web servers were configured. It has become the norm for web pages to be built and delivered on the fly with content management systems (CMS). These application servers build every web page from a database of elements including pictures, video, and text content.

CMS systems include the popular WordPress for blogs or the open source Joomla and Drupal for more sophisticated websites. Each uses PHP scripts to pull information from a SQL database such as MySQL or MicrosoftSQL. (PHP is a high-level programming language, SQL stands for Structured Query Language.) The websites in Estonia succumbed quickly to denial of service attacks, not because the web server could not handle the number of requests, but because the back-end databases were not designed to respond to repeated floods of requests.

The system administrators for the downed Estonian websites quickly realized the flaw in their architecture and threw together a large number of cache servers to store static copies of web pages built from the back-end databases. The primary tool for doing this was SQUID, an open source server product designed to store and serve up content that is requested repeatedly. The SQUID "farms" put in place within 72 hours brought most of Estonia's beleaguered websites back online.

AFTERMATH

The cyber attacks on Estonia were a pivotal moment in the rising tide of cyber warfare. NATO was called upon to consider the question: "At what point does a cyber attack become an act of war thus invoking Article V of the NATO treaty that requires member nations to come to the aid of the party under attack?" And, if an act of war has been committed what is the appropriate response? One response was to establish the NATO Cooperative Cyber Defence Centre of Excellence (CCDCOE) in a repurposed Estonian army barracks not too far from the new resting place of the Bronze Soldier. This is the first time a cooperative effort to study cyber war has been created, although the Chinese and Russians have military science academies that study modern methods of warfare. In addition, several think tanks have considered the consequences of Information Warfare (IW). Estonia now plays a leading role in the European Union for cyber defense. It hosted the EU Ministries Conference on Critical Information Protection in 2009 and holds an annual conference on cyberwar. (They have to use the National Opera because it is the only venue in Tallinn that is big enough.)

Estonia was the first country to experience the wrath of the Russian cyber crowd. It was not the last, as we shall see in the next chapter.

CYBERWAR CUTS A
SWATH THROUGH
EASTERN EUROPE

Estonia was only the beginning. Pro-Russian-attributed attacks against Chechen separatists, the Ukraine, Lithuania, and Radio Free Europe preceded and followed the attacks on Estonia. The stage is set for cyberwar.

The reason they lost is they did not know how to riot.

—Dulles

We leave Estonia arming itself as best it can against the great Russian bear on its border and turn to several other incidents that involve Russia and its ex-satellite states. The stories are remarkable in their similarity.

In the early days of the Internet, during the war that broke out between Serbia and NATO, rebels in Serbia demonstrated one of the first uses of the Internet to gain support for their cause. They used their own sites to post their separatist messages and engaged in attacks against NATO sites. In March 1999 they took down NATO's main web server hosted in Brussels with a Ping flood. (See chapter 7 to learn about Ping floods.) This was a wake-up call to NATO, which had a staff of only two people managing information security. The Happy99 virus, which had first appeared a month before, was also used to target and disable

NATO's e-mail server, causing a serious interruption to communication within the organization managing the conflict in Kosovo.

Writing in her paper "War.com: The Internet and Psychological Operations," Major Angela Maria Lunga states:

> Both the Serb government (www.serbiainfo.com) and Kosovo Liberation Army (www.kosova.com) are using Web sites and e-mail to make their cases. The Chechen site (kavkaz.org), run by a former information minister, learned from the Serbs and features video footage of Russian bombing and shelling. As a result, Moscow launched the Russian Information Center (www.gov.ru).[1]

The last major war fought in the twentieth century was between Russia and Chechnya. The Islamist rebels of Chechnya followed the path of Serbia in its war against NATO by using the Internet to post news and pictures of Russian actions that were being denied by Russia. Western news media used the sites Kavkaz.com, hosted in the United States, and Chechenpress.com as sources of information otherwise unobtainable. A report posted October 9, 1999, by Radio Free Europe:

> Last week, Moscow officials denied that Russian forces had attacked a bus carrying refugees and killed many of them. But before that report could be aired on central Russian television, the Chechens used their Internet website to post photographs of the incident.

And:

> Speaking to journalists last week, Putin openly acknowledged that Moscow was playing catch-up on this battlefield: "We surrendered this terrain some time ago," he said, "but now we are entering the game again." The prime minister's remarks came on the heels of reports that Russia's evolving national security concept now calls for tightened control over the media during crisis situations.

And:

> In recent weeks, the Russian government responded on a number of fronts. It has tried to close down the most important of the Chechen web sites—www.kavkaz.org—and even sought help from Western governments to that end.[2]

Perhaps the status of Putin's "catch-up" was demonstrated in 2002, when Kavkaz.com and Chechenpress.com were attacked by denial of service attacks and the domain name registration of kavkaz.com was hijacked. The editor of Kavkaz.com claimed that these were the direct result of Russian FSB (the Russian Intelligence Agency) actions. The battle between opposing hackers continued, with similar attacks occurring against Russian news sites. In 2004 the Maslan.A virus was created that targeted Chechenpress.com and Kavkazcenter.com (the replacement for Kavkaz.org.) A Finnish anti-virus vendor, F-Secure, reported the virus was of Russian origin.

Ukraine has had a tumultuous history marked by invasions from Goths, Huns, Turks, Mongols, Poles, Cossacks, Lithuania, Germany, and the Soviet Union. After World War II the Ukraine was subjected to the ravishment of Stalinism including mass starvation and deportation of dissidents.

Independence came in August 1991, and the leadership of Ukraine, Belarus, and Russia formally dissolved the Soviet Union in December 1991. After Russia, Ukraine is the largest and most powerful economy of the post-Soviet states.

The Ukraine played an important role in the rise of crowd sourced attacks. (See chapter 8.) The rigged elections of 2004 led to a nonviolent uprising, the Orange Revolution, which in turn led to new elections. The opposition leader, Viktor Yushchenko, became president. The prime minister, Yuliya Tymoshenko, is a vocal opponent of Russian hegemony.

In January 2007 the Eurasian Youth Union broke into and disabled the official website of President Yushchenko. And in October of 2007 the presidential website www.president.gov.ua came under extended DDoS for several days. The Eurasian Youth Movement, a group that opposed Ukraine's intentions of joining NATO, claimed credit for this attack.[3]

Radio Free Europe, the U.S.-backed news source established to broadcast into the Soviet Union, and still in operation today throughout Europe, suffered a similar attack in March of 2008. It was the anniversary of Chernobyl, the disastrous meltdown of a nuclear pile in Ukraine. Much of the radioactive cloud from the disaster rained down on Belarus, a neighbor to the north. Planned demonstrations in remembrance of the catastrophe were opposed by the pro-Russian president of Belarus, who is blamed for instigating an attack on Radio Free Europe's Belarus website and, shortly after, seven other RFE sites in Eastern Europe.

Lithuania, in an acknowledgment of its independent status, passed legislation calling for the elimination of Soviet era symbols from parks, public buildings, and websites in late June 2008. The new law prohibited the public display of the Soviet flag, military uniforms, and the five-pointed Soviet star, as well as the playing of the Soviet national anthem. This incurred the wrath of pro-Russia nationalists, who attacked websites of government agencies, political parties, and businesses, defacing them with the hammer-and-sickle symbol and five-pointed stars. Included in the list of 300 defaced websites were a car dealership and a grocery chain, demonstrating that cyberwar can quickly splash over into the realm of commerce.

One common element of all of these pro-Russian attacks is the lack of evidence tying the government of Russia to them, even though they align with Russia's desire to exert a controlling influence over Eastern Europe. Solving the attribution problem is a task that nations are going to have to concentrate on if they are going to be able to provide for their own defense and make appropriate responses to incursions against their information assets.

We have seen how warring factions engage in mutual attacks against each other's websites as they attempt to silence the messages of their opponents. Estonia was the most egregious event with simultaneous riots and diplomatic missions. What about cyber attacks that accompany an actual invasion? Let's talk about Georgia.

GEORGIA: THE FIRST CYBERWAR

Russia used crowd sourced DDoS, coupled with network outages in neighboring countries, in conjunction with a physical attack against Georgia in 2008. This is the first conflict that meets the definition of cyberwar. The repercussions of this incident still reverberate today.

It needs but one foe to breed a war, and those who have not swords can still die upon them.

—J. R. R. Tolkien

The first occurrence of cyberwar was August 7, 2008, with the outbreak of simultaneous military and cyber attacks against the country of Georgia. All of the military thinking on information warfare and the Revolution in Military Affairs in China and the subsequent incursions into Western computer systems, and all of the crowd sourced attacks attributed to Russian instigation were only precursors to this first invasion via cyber space.

Georgia is a small mountainous country in the region that separates Europe and Asia. To the south lies Turkey and to the north, Russia. Stalin was an ethnic Georgian. Like so many of the former Soviet Socialist Republics, Georgia has suffered centuries of turmoil marked by invasions, pogroms, and internal upheaval. It was ruled by the Russian czars throughout the 1800s and briefly experienced independence after the Bolshevik Revolution of October 1917, but was occupied by the Red Army soon after that and became a Soviet state. In 1991 it declared its independence once again as the Soviet Union dissolved.

After some internal conflicts and attempts at establishing a government, the polyglot Mikheil Saakashvili was elected to the presidency. Misha, as he is called in Georgia, is an American-educated lawyer. He had gone abroad to attend Columbia and George Washington Universities. In early 1995 he left an internship with the New York law firm of Patterson Belknap Webb & Tyler to return to the newly democratic Georgia and enter politics. He is fluent in Georgian, Ukrainian, Russian, and English. He is reported to speak Ossetian (an Eastern-Iranian dialect) and Spanish as well. In 2008 he was 41 years old.

In 2008 Georgia was in conflict with Russia over the status of two of its northern regions, Abkhazia and South Ossetia. Russia supported these regions in their attempts to become independent, and Georgia was trying to hold on to these breakaway territories.

An interesting series of events led up to the Russian military incursion into South Ossetia and Abkhazia in August 2008. Georgia had just had its application to join NATO postponed. An alliance with NATO would have meant an attack on its territories would necessitate the involvement of the other treaty members. Vladimir Putin, now prime minister of Russia, was attending the 2008 Summer Olympics in Beijing. He is pictured in news reports sitting next to U.S. President George W. Bush watching a sporting event while the actual invasion began.

Cyber attacks began against Georgia the month before kinetic attacks. On July 20, 2008, the ShadowServer Foundation, an independent research organization, documented a carefully orchestrated attack against Saakashvili's presidential website. They observed that a botnet never seen before called Machbot was communicating with a command and control server in the United States to obtain instructions for a denial of service attack. The commands they saw were:

```
flood http www.president.gov.ge/
flood tcp www.president.gov.ge
flood icmp www.president.gov.ge
```

These commands caused the botnet to flood the presidential website with http, tcp, and icmp packets, making it unavailable for a 24-hour period. Other websites hosted on the same server were down as well. One of them was also associated with the government of Georgia: the Social Assistance and Employment State Agency website (www.saesa.gov.ge).

On August 7, 2008, the situation in South Ossetia became confused as Georgia claimed that South Ossetian rebels were firing missiles into Georgian settlements while Russia claimed that several of their in-place "peacekeeping" troops were killed. It now appears that Georgia was, indeed, the first to mobilize and move its tanks and troops across its border into its South Ossetian territory. Russia was prepared and reacted quickly in the early hours of August 8 by sending tanks across their border with South Ossetia through the Russian-controlled Roki Tunnel and launching air strikes against military targets within Georgia proper.

Massive cyber attacks were launched against Georgian websites on the evening of August 7, before Russia invaded. The effects, regardless of who launched the cyber attacks, were to disable the websites that Georgia used to communicate with its populace and the world as well as the websites of Georgian banks and other ministries. This disrupted communications to the outside world. A veil was drawn over the theater of operations during a military invasion. Saakashvili was adept at using his English websites to make his case to the world that Georgia was struggling against Russian hegemony. As war broke out that voice was silenced.

Many researchers have delved into the cyber events of that August. Their findings are cataloged here.

On the evening of August 7, the website of the president of Georgia (www.president.gov.ge) was commandeered and defaced with a slideshow of images showing President Saakashvili juxtaposed with images of Hitler in similar poses. This was a level of graphic artistry that had to be prepared in advance.

The ShadowServer Foundation observed new botnet attacks against several Georgian websites including www.parliament.ge and president .gov.ge using http floods. The command and control server at IP address 79.135.167.22 was located in Turkey.

A website, StopGeorgia.com, attributed to the Russian Business Network (RBN), posted instructions for targeting 36 different servers in

Georgia. A Google translation of the page provided by Jart Armin, who maintains the RBNExploit.com website, had the following statement:

> We—the representatives of Russian hako-underground will not tolerate provocation by the Georgian in all its manifestations. We want to live in a free world, but exist in a free-aggression and Setevom space.

The targets enumerated were:

www.parliament.ge	www.rustavi2.com.ge
www.assitancegeorgia.org.ge	www.opentext.org.ge
www.cec.gov.ge	www.svobodnaya-gruzia.com
www.mdf.org.ge	www.sanet.ge
www.corruption.ge	www.messenger.com.ge
www.constcourt.gov.ge	georgianmessenger.blogspot.com
www.insurance.caucasus.net	www.primenewsonline.com
www.mc.gov.ge	www.presidpress.gov.ge
www.nsc.gov.ge	www.sakinform.ge
www.supremecourt.ge	www.sakarvelo.ru
www.iberiapac.ge	www.internews.ge
www.court.gov.ge	www.internews.org.ge
www.civil.ge	www.interpressnews.ge
georgia.usembassy.gov tbilisivisa @state.gov	www.internet.ge
ukingeorgia.fco.gov.uk/en	www.stream.ge
www.all.ge	newsgeorgia.ge
www.geres.ge	presa.ge
	www.medianews.ge

The organizations targeted included U.S. and UK embassies in Tbilisi; Georgian Parliament; Georgian Supreme Court; Ministry of Foreign Affairs; various newspapers, television, and other media resources; the Central Election Commission; and even a news blog hosted at blogspot.com.

In addition, traceroutes from the United States showed that access to the websites of the Georgian Ministry of Defense (www.mod.gov .ge), the Georgian Ministry of Foreign Affairs (www.mof.gov.ge), and the presidential website were blocked at Ttnet (AS9121), a service provider in Turkey that, according to GeorgiaUpdate.gov.ge, "is associated with AbdAllah_Internet, which is linked with cybercrime hosting such as thecanadianmeds.com. These are known Russian Business Network routes."

Traffic from the Ukraine to the Ministry of Foreign Affairs was redirected through Bryansk.ru to a forged page as well.

Analysis of these attacks provided at www.georgiaupdate.gov.ge attributes them to the Russian Business Network (RBN). The RBN is a shady organization that has been blamed for the original CoolWeb-Search spyware, massive spam operations, an elaborate web-based attack network based on IFrames vulnerabilities in Internet Explorer, extensive phishing attacks, and the operation of a global carding operation connected to Russian organized crime. It is supposedly headquartered in St. Petersburg, Russia, and some of its members are former KGB operatives. Many innovations in creating malware that harvests computers to enlist them in botnets are also attributed to the RBN.

The *GeorgiaUpdate* website provides the following details.

Stopgeorgia.ru which provided the above targets and hacking tools for independent hackers to attack them was hosted by AS36351(an Autonomous System Number used by ARIN to allocate IP address space) belonging to Softlayer of Plano, Texas.

Stopgeorgia.info was hosted by NETDIRECT (AS28753) in Frankfurt, Germany, as well as APOLLO LATTELEKOM APOLLO (AS12578) in Latvia.

The link back to the Russian Business Network (RBN) was provided by the clues left in the domain name registration (WHOIS database), which reads:

• Sponsoring Registrar: EstDomains, Inc.
  Registrant: Domain Manager, Protect Details, Inc, Street1: 29 Kompozitorov St., Saint Petersburg, RU, Phone:+7.8129342271

They go on to point a finger at two people they claim are part of the RBN: Alexandr A. Boykov and Andrey Smirnov of St. Petersburg, Russia.

The international reactions to the cyber attacks on Georgia are worth noting. By August 13 Estonia deployed two cyber advisors from the

Estonian CERT to assist with defense and presumably share what they had learned when they were under attack from Russia the previous year. Meanwhile Poland provided space on its own presidential website for Saakashvili to post updates on the developing situation.

Another interesting story developed when the owner of a web-hosting service in the United Systems, Tulip Systems, just happened to be vacationing in Georgia when the hostilities broke out. Nino Doijashvili, a native-born Georgian, reached out to the government and arranged to move president.gov.ge and rustavi2.com, the TV station, to her company's servers on August 9. In an interview on August 12 with a reporter from *Agence France Presse*, Tom Burling, another Tulip executive, said that their engineers had been working around the clock dealing with the floods of attacks that were now turned like a fire hose on their hosting service located in, of all places, Atlanta, Georgia. They were experiencing over 68,000 web requests per second even after Russia had called a cessation to hostilities on August 12, the day of the interview.

Tulip Systems, by interceding on behalf of the beleaguered Georgian government, had interjected itself into a cyberwar and exposed the rest of their customer base to attacks intended for Georgian sites. They also brought U.S. networks into the fray. This type of collateral damage brings the threat of repercussions from state-sponsored attacks closer to every business and network connected entity.

While the initial attacks on Georgia petered out over the next several days, there was another massive DDoS launched against the Ministry of Foreign Affairs website on August 27. Quoting once again from GeorgiaUpdate.gov.ge:

> The attacks peaked at approx 0.5 million network packets per second, and up to 200–250 Mbits per second in bandwidth. . . . The attacks mainly consisted of HTTP queries to the http://mfa.gov.ge website. These were requests for the main page script with randomly generated parameters. These requests were generated to overload the web server in a way where every single request would need significant CPU time."

The suddenness of this attack and the fact that it tailed off quickly after only about six hours indicates that this was a botnet under the control of a single agent. The attack took the target website off-line and demonstrated that whatever defensive measures Georgia had been able to put in place since the war were still ineffective.

Unfortunately, the story does not end there. The following year, on the anniversary of the Georgian war, another attack occurred. This one had global repercussions. It involved a Georgian blogger who had come to be a vocal critic of Russia and a supporter of Georgia. He went by his screen name Cyxymu. On August 8, 2009, a massive distributed denial of service attack was launched against Cyxymu's blog at LiveJournal .com, along with his Twitter account, his Blogger.com page, and his Facebook page. All four of these services suffered outages, with Twitter seeing the most damage as it became completely unavailable to its 20 million users for over three hours.

The fact that four of the Internet's largest online communities could not withstand an attack of this nature demonstrates that even the huge investment those services have made in infrastructure and network connectivity to serve the demands of their huge user bases can succumb to DDoS. Twitter even uses the on-demand computing infrastructure of Amazon's cloud services to allow it to stay stable while it adds millions of users a month. Large Web 2.0 services such as Twitter and Facebook will be studying the attack of August 2009 to discover what went wrong and how to defend themselves from similar attacks in the future.

The successful attacks on Georgia's networks, banks, and key government websites during an outbreak of physical hostilities has changed the threat landscape for all nations that rely on computing and networks to conduct commerce, communicate with their citizens, and interface with their critical infrastructure. They now have to assume that any future armed conflict will have coincident cyber attack vectors. This means not an arms race but a race to implement defenses before they are called upon.

LESSONS LEARNED FROM GEORGIA

Many of the simple security measures enumerated in this book will have to be followed and special defenses against cyber infiltration and DDoS will have to be deployed. This means several things:

Most organizations responsible for their country's defense will have to reorganize to include special forces that have the expertise to deploy and manage cyber defenses. Many countries and even militaries have treated IT resources the same way they treat the production and servicing of uniforms: something to be outsourced to government contractors because it has little to do with fighting wars. That has changed and the activity to address their lack of cyber war capability will have to be ramped up quickly.

Finding military personnel to achieve this ramp-up will be difficult. IT security has traditionally found its practitioners from all walks of life. Only since 2000 have there been widely available degree programs in information security. Most IT security experts are self-taught or came up through the engineering departments of large businesses and IT security vendors. Because the rising threat levels have made them scarce resources who command attractive salaries, it is not likely they will drop everything to join a government bureaucracy.

Perhaps the model for finding and training a cyber corps can be borrowed from that which is used to build the ranks of other specialists, in particular armed forces medical personnel. The level of skill, intelligence, and education needed to get a medical practitioner up to speed reflects the same levels needed for IT security personnel.

In October 2009 the Secretary of DHS Janet Napolitano announced the U.S. Department of Homeland Security would hire 1,000 "security experts" just to address the shortfall they had already identified. No definition of a security expert was provided nor was an indication of what their roles would be. A telling internal request for information memo was published at the U.S. Office of Personnel Management to ask various departments to provide titles and functions of cyber security roles in existence today. From that data, it is assumed, they hope to standardize job descriptions and pay grades. That is just one indication of the monumental task facing military organizations. Post-Georgia they know they have a void to fill, but because they have not gone to battle in an all-out cyberwar they are guessing at what will be needed.

One action that will help immediately is to create research functions, even establishing separate labs on the order of Sandia, Livermore, or Oak Ridge. The government must keep in mind that in this Internet age all researchers do not need to be housed in one facility surrounded by fences and armed guards. They can work from wherever they reside, as long as adequate security measures are taken! That model might be hard to swallow for a system that has grown up around elected officials whose purpose is to see large investments of federal funds directed toward their constituencies. But perhaps it is time to try something new. These research functions of existing departments or brand new organizations would have the tasks of quantifying the current threat, evaluating the defensive posture of the existing branches of the military and government, and identifying new methods of improving those postures quickly. The suggestions in chapters 3 ("Countering Cyber Espionage") and 15 ("Repercussions") would be a good place to start.

Imagine the computer models that would have to be built to predict the effect of a globally dispersed, centrally controlled, DDoS on a network with over 1,000 access points. Creating the computing infrastructure to model that and measure the effects of various defense scenarios would task any research and development facility. As is usual in the case of pure research, such efforts would inevitably lead to dividends as new supercomputers, more efficient network devices, and new security tools made their way to the private sector.

In addition to the need for more cyber-savvy personnel and more research and development, nations are beginning to recognize the need for new treaties and conventions to curtail the use of cyber weapons. There is a natural reticence on the part of military organizations to hamper their war-fighting ability with international conventions. After all, their task is to wage war with the objective of winning. Restricting the available weapons seems counterproductive. Yet, horrific weapons such as poison gas, biological weapons, personnel land mines, and nuclear weapons have been subject to international treaties, and it is reasonable to assume that cyber weapons will be as well.

The governments of Estonia and Georgia called on NATO to recognize the attacks they suffered as acts of war under article five of the NATO Treaty. This would mean that NATO would be compelled to respond with conventional means (tanks, rockets, troops) to attacks that even now have not been attributed to Russian leaders with enough assurance to warrant such a response. Nations will need to put cyber attacks and appropriate responses on the table as their diplomatic delegations plan future meetings of the G-20 and ASEAN.

Perhaps one guiding precept would be the creation of cyber treaties that would bind one country to the other participants but be limited to cyber responses only. If one country came under attack the other treaty signatories could offer people, bandwidth, access to networks, and hosting services to help the victim survive and recover with minimum disruption. That precedent has already been set by the help rendered to Georgia from Estonia, Poland, and a small hosting provider in the United States. This is also how the global community of network operators already interact during times of crisis, be it an accidental route announcement from Pakistan (such as the YouTube incident described in chapter 7) or a targeted attack from cyber criminals.

Post-Georgia, taking a moment to review the impact that technological change has had on warfighting will help shed light on the current problem of how military organizations (and their governments and businesses that rely on the Internet) should respond to the now evident threat of cyberwar.

CONFLICT CAUSES CHANGE

In this chapter we introduce the thesis that cyber warfare is an extension of the development of war. Conflict brings about change. Technological, military, and geopolitical balances are reset.

> *It seemed to me proven that our rebellion had an unassailable base, guarded not only from attack, but from the fear of attack.*
>
> —T. E. Lawrence

While the travesty of the 1916 Battle of the Somme is hard to comprehend in its enormity, it is notable for the rapid development of warfare that occurred because of it. The French army and the British Expeditionary Force had arranged themselves across a 25-mile front facing the heavily entrenched German army. On the Allied side was a hastily constructed force of English volunteers exhorted to fight by patriotic calls to duty and promises that those that "joined together would fight together." In the space of four months and at a cost that exceeded one million casualties on both sides, the tools and techniques of modern warfare advanced at a pace never before seen. The parallels between change in warfare and change in cyber security are worth exploring. Just as all of IT security is developed and deployed in response to attacks, warfare over the centuries has changed with each major conflict.

The Battle of the Somme was the defining conflict of World War I. At the outbreak of the war in 1914, the German army, consisting of reservists who had been preparing for war for years, flooded across Belgium and penetrated to within thirty miles of Paris before being stalled and turned back by the French army. The French managed to hold the Germans at bay for eighteen months while Britain raised an army, converted its manufacturing capability to guns, shells, and rifles, and deployed to the front in northern France.

The use of massive amounts of artillery was one of the elements that contributed to the horrors of trench warfare. Both sides placed batteries well behind the lines that could toss shells from guns with bores up to 18 inches in diameter. The Allied forces used 3,000 heavy artillery to pound the German line for eight days before the Battle of the Somme was launched on July 1, 1916. The distances were so great that both sides quickly invented methods of ranging on the other's guns based on the delay between seeing the muzzle flash and hearing the sound of the remote gun, much as one follows the approach of a summer thunderstorm by counting the seconds between seeing the flash of lightning and hearing the thunder. If a spotter could both see the muzzle flash and determine the distance, they had their elevation and direction to target the enemy gun.

Just prior to launching what became known as "the big push," the French also determined that the best tactic for using heavy artillery was to engage in a series of "lifts." They would pound the front lines of the German trenches for days at a time. Then when the whistles blew and the Allied troops came up out of their trenches the gunnery officers would elevate their guns to cause the shells to fall farther behind the German lines, leaving the intervening space between the armies' lines free of bombardment while it was being crossed, and simultaneously preventing reinforcements from moving forward from the German rear. As the attackers progressed the guns would be "lifted" once again to pummel the German army in retreat. These new techniques met with limited success because of command and control issues. Communication between the front and the gunners was by underground telephone lines supplemented by messenger, sometimes even by carrier pigeon. A delay in the advance could mean that by the time the Allied troops got to the German front line the trenches were fully manned and the first wave would be utterly repulsed.

The Germans introduced two weapons of modern warfare with limited success: flamethrowers and poison gas. The British quickly responded with their own versions of these weapons. Chlorine gas forced both sides to equip their forces with protective gear, causing them to be weighed down with gas masks in addition to the 60 pounds of guns, ammo, and supplies they carried with them.

The two most important additions to regular warfare that evolved out of the Battle of the Somme were machine guns and tanks.

At the outset of the battle, the Allied forces had four machine guns per division. By the end of the battle four months later each division was supported by a specialized machine gun corps that was deployed in four companies of four Vickers machine guns devoted to each of three brigades in a division, or 48 total machine guns per division.

In addition to the important change of creating a specialized machine gun corps, tactics were developed rapidly. At the outset of the Battle of the Somme machine guns were regarded as effective weapons for stopping hoards of attackers from fixed positions. But the British had to be on the offensive against the German line. They threw the machine gunners in with the regular infantry thinking they could help consolidate positions once they were obtained. By the end of July the British Machine Gun Corps had developed tactics that included the first use of "indirect fire." Much like artillery, the machine guns were carefully pointed at precalculated spots on a map in continuous fire, creating a hail of bullets that in one case tallied 900,000 rounds fired from ten guns over a 12-hour period and led to one of the few British victories during the long months of the battle.

Tanks were famously introduced during the Battle of the Somme. While they had the predictable breakdowns and snafus—only 25 of 50 brought to the front actually engaged, the shock value and the effective use of tanks supporting an infantry advance forever changed the modern battlefield. Unfortunately for the British and French, just how much mechanized infantry changed the face of warfare was not recognized until Hitler's armored brigades overran France and pushed the British Expeditionary Force into the English Channel at the outset of World War II.

To further make the argument that innovation in techniques of warfare occur during a conflict it is well worth turning to another front of World War I, where guerrilla warfare techniques were being born in the mind of Lieutenant T. E. Lawrence. In his epic account of the *Revolt in the Desert*, Lawrence of Arabia tells of a cathartic moment that changed not only the outcome of the British-supported war against the Turks but impacted the operations of insurgencies ever since.

Lawrence had been with the combined British and Arab armies in Wejh on the coast of the Red Sea. He took a small band of Arabs inland to hook up with a tribe of Bedouins whom he was to exhort into harassing the main railway along which the Turks were retreating as they slowly abandoned Medina. That trip, poetically depicted by Lawrence with a painterly description of lava flows, sparse vegetation, and undulating terrain, culminates in one of the most wrenching moments in twentieth-century literature as Lawrence executes one of his party for committing murder.

Wracked by dysentery picked up in Wehj and suffering from boils from his camel ride, Lawrence collapses at his destination and falls into a feverish dream-state, where he draws upon his not inconsiderable knowledge of war history and strategy to reformulate the purpose and technique of the Arab Revolution. Up until this epiphany, the Arab irregulars were considered an adjunct to the British effort. Traditional ideas on flanking, cutting supply lines, and supporting regular troops were the thought of the day. In his almost delusional state Lawrence envisioned Arabia as a vast impenetrable territory. If the Turks encountered a land that was defended within every square mile rather than on defined fronts of traditional warfare they would not be able to command the resources to dominate that land. This idea of dispersed defense fit the temperament and natural deployment of the Arab tribes. It did not fit the British concept of warfare at the time, but from that moment Lawrence set into motion forces that even today are felt in the makeup of the Mideast.

Incidentally, Lawrence's innovation can be translated into concepts of cyber defense that will be explored shortly.

The Battle of the Somme and the history of innovation in warfare from the introduction of the longbow to the hydrogen bomb is not a metaphor for the developments of IT security. Rather, IT security is an extension of the evolution of warfare. Viewing security from this perspective lends a focus that, if applied, can shed light on the rise of cyber attacks and provide guidance as governments try to respond to them.

Many people in the security industry are frustrated by the reactionary approach most entities take to network security. Defenses against viruses, worms, spam, spyware, targeted attacks, data loss, and distributed denial of service are not deployed until after those attacks have occurred. Every organization must learn firsthand about loss of intellectual property, brand impacts of having their website defaced, and the cost of lost business when they are subject to denial of service attacks. The ultimate frustration arises when organizations do not even learn from incidents that impact others in their own space.

TJX, the multibillion-dollar retailer and the poster child for how not to handle a data breach incident, announced in January 2007 that their database of credit card information had been stolen. The *Wall Street Journal* reported that hackers had broken into one of their retail outlets in Minneapolis through an unprotected wireless access point. This is the exact same methodology used by a couple of hackers in 2003 to break into a Lowe's home improvement store in Southfield, Michigan. The Lowe's incident was widely reported at the time. This author took a personal interest because the FBI stakeout that led to the arrest of the hackers ensnared one of his former employees. (He was eventually exonerated, in part due to the fact that, being the geek he is, he had configured a server and web page to report his geolocation at all times and he could demonstrate that he was not present at the time of the break-in.)

Despite the widespread warnings of vulnerabilities in how WiFi was implemented, TJX failed to review and correct the way they protected their perimeter and incurred data loss costs of over $200 million.

Another widespread practice, at least within the United States, is for banks and stock trading firms to allow access to online financial services with only user names and passwords. All an attacker needs is to get those simple credentials. As attacks against banks escalate there is much to be learned from studying previous attacks against banks in other regions.

In early 2003 the banks in Istanbul noticed a rise in stolen accounts. Istanbul had yet to benefit from the wave of deregulation of telecom infrastructure that was making Internet access affordable for many households around the world. Therefore, Internet cafes that provided relatively speedy access at affordable rates were how most banking customers accessed their accounts. The banks quickly learned that they were in a contest with cyber thieves who were installing keystroke logging software on the computers in the Internet cafes. Simple usernames and passwords were the first casualty. The banks investigated and deployed authentication technology that would display an on-screen keyboard that their customers would click using a mouse. Within days the attackers had modified their malicious software to also record small screen captures around the cursor whenever the mouse was clicked, thus obtaining each character of the username and password. Turkish banks were quickly forced to use one-time password schemes to protect their online business model. Even if an attacker captured the current password, they would have no idea what the password would be the next time the account was accessed.

U.S. banks and stock trading firms are slow to make the switch to strong authentication because of the fear of introducing too much friction to the online banking paradigm. Online banking is a money saver for the banks and they fear that too many customers would reject the complexity of using a onetime password token, card swipe machine, or cell phone-based authentication. Instead, financial services firms treat the losses from identity theft as a cost of doing business, which may be reasonable from a pure accounting and risk management perspective, but has an unintended consequence.

There is a rapid evolution of attacks against bank accounts. Phishing attacks delivered by e-mail have become increasingly sophisticated, to the point where methods have been demonstrated that can circumvent the use of strong authentication.

Rather than take protective action, banks have chosen to guarantee their customers' assets. If a customer loses money the banks invariably refund the lost amount. They calculate that the bottom line is best served by taking this approach. But what the banks are actually doing is funding cyber criminals. Every time a criminal successfully absconds with funds more criminals are encouraged to copy his success. The enriched criminal moves on to his next exploit, this time perhaps to attempt to extort money from the bank with a denial of service attack funded in part with money stolen from the bank! This battle is not over. Cyber criminals are developing the tools of this conflict, widespread botnets, DDoS attacks, and spyware used by any party looking to steal information or target attacks against an adversary.

It is easiest to understand how organizations do not build in defenses until a conflict or attack is already under way by studying the history of viruses and worms. Even though the vulnerability that allowed Robert Morris's worm to spread was theorized several years before he launched it, no one took the effort to configure Unix computers to avoid it until after the worm had had its way. Today, owners of Apple computers are smug in a sense of false security because there are no widespread worms or attacks against them: even though Apple computers are fraught with easily targeted vulnerabilities and there are anti-virus programs available, few Apple computers are protected.

The vulnerability in Microsoft's Internet Information Server (IIS), which led to the spread of CodeRed as well as Nimda, was an instance of change wrought by conflict. These worms were escalations in capability with Nimda being a sophisticated multiheaded worm with five avenues of attack, one of which targeted IIS machines that had previously been infected by CodeRed. The results from these attacks were improved patch management and deployment of Intrusion Prevention Systems (IPS).

The SQL Slammer worm gave rise to protective measures exercised by Internet backbone carriers who started to invest in technology that would allow them to recognize changes in traffic patterns and apply filters to eradicate the offending traffic.

The rise of spyware is another example of reactionary security measures. Spammers discovered they could write code that engaged in relatively low impact threats such as pop-up ads, redirecting searches, and tracking browsing patterns, and that they could hide that code in so-called ad-supported software packages such as screen savers, flapping butterfly animated cursors, or weather toolbars. The anti-virus vendors did not recognize adware as a threat because it used social engineering in the form of an elaborate ruse to get the user's permission to be installed on each machine. It did not fit their definition of a virus. The battle with spyware writers was most remarkable in the case of Cool Web Search (CWS), reportedly created in Eastern Europe by a nefarious criminal organization called the Russian Business Network (RBN). As anti-spyware programs were modified to recognize each version of CWS, a new version would be released. At one point the code was modified for every new download and installation.

Ultimately the industry reacted, laws were passed, and spyware is no longer the scourge it was. Anti-spyware capabilities have been built into most anti-virus products.

The current front is in the area of DDoS and espionage. These are threats that many organizations are not even aware they face. Evidence of successful espionage against the Pentagon's e-mail servers, malware distributed by USB thumb drives that targets military bases, and the theft of a terabyte of design data for the new U.S. Joint Strike Fighter, the F-35, is fueling changes within the U.S. Department of Homeland Security. As appropriate defenses are deployed it is important to understand that warfare has undergone constant change over the centuries and that we are in fact entering yet another phase of rapid change as network infrastructure has been deployed to most military, government, and critical infrastructure arenas, thus opening them up for attack over the very networks that are making commerce, communication, and command and control more effective.

It is tempting to think of IT security in terms of a front. In those terms a cyber front must be armed with defensive weapons deployed to best advantage. But there is no physical equivalent to the Internet. Thinking of it in terms of traditional warfare will not lead to any productive conclusions. General Kevin P. Chilton, who heads up the U.S. Strategic Command (STRATCOM) has a better way of looking at what the military likes to call "cyberspace."

As cyberwar and cyber defense become major topics of discussion, various agencies within the United States are struggling to define their own responsibility. STRATCOM is already in charge of aerial refueling, airborne communications, ballistic missile submarines, strategic bomber and reconnaissance aircraft, and land-based intercontinental ballistic missiles. These charges are outside the traditional realm of the army (land), navy (sea), and air force (air), branches of military organization that have not changed—except with the addition of the air force—in a thousand years. To accommodate a domain such as space that is global in nature and covers all the other domains, STRATCOM was formed. It is jointly operated by the three branches.

General Chilton wishes to extend the idea of domains to cyberspace and treat it much like space, communications, and intercontinental ballistic missiles. Treating cyberspace as a domain has merit over treating the Internet piecemeal as a series of new threats and weapons. But if the history of warfare and the equally relevant history of the development of IT security measures are studied there is one thing that is certain. Change, and the eventual adoption of military operations to cyberwar will come about during conflict. That change will be directed by leaders who will have to make decisions at the time. Some of those decisions, like changing how machine guns are deployed at the battalion level, will be effective. Others, like using bulky, fuel-gobbling flamethrowers, will be discarded. Military leaders can observe conflict today in many microcosms and learn from the near-real-time developments in IT security. They can conduct exercises and simulations in hopes of predicting what the future holds. But real conflict will change the tools, organization, and methods of warfare in the cyber domain.

Perhaps military theorists should go through the thought process that led Lieutenant Lawrence to his conclusions and his dramatic innovation in warfare. There is a close parallel between Lawrence's concept of a hardened interior defended by its natives at the fine level of a square mile and what is becoming recognized as an appropriate model for information security.

Effective information security is achieved through hardening. Data at rest is encrypted and access is controlled at the document level. Operating systems and applications are quickly patched. Protective firewalls, anti-virus, and anti-spyware reside on every host. Systems are configured to only execute explicitly identified actions (white listing). Network protections are deployed at every juncture to filter out attacks. Strong authentication is used to ensure that access controls are enforced. Telecom providers are able to filter attacks at their edge to prevent DDoS attacks. Activity is monitored to identify new attacks.

The remaining question is how to organize a military operation to effectively conduct information warfare. How can a government best organize its country's people, telecom, power grid, water, first responders, and banking infrastructure to survive an attack? Because the Internet and, in fact, most IT assets are not the responsibility of the government, cyber preparedness is harder to conceptualize than missile defense or satellite reconnaissance.

In the next chapters we apply the lessons of history to the idea of making best use of cyber weapons to wage war, and how nations around the world are arming themselves for cyberwar.

FOUR PILLARS OF CYBERWAR

━━━━━━━━━━━━━━━━━━━━━━━ ∞∞ ━━━━━━━━━━━━━━━━━━━━━━━

This chapter introduces the four pillars of cyberwar: effective means of gaining total information dominance through intelligence, technology, logistics, and command. It is both a guide and a warning to nations preparing for cyberwar.

━━━━━━━━━━━━━━━━━━━━━━━ ∞∞ ━━━━━━━━━━━━━━━━━━━━━━━

There could be no honor in sure success, but much might be wrested from a sure defeat.

—T. E. Lawrence

There are four pillars to the cyberwar realm: intelligence, technology, logistics, and command. Cyber warfare is a component of the ongoing struggle between philosophies of politics, governance, and markets to be waged by opposing interests be they nation versus nation, law enforcement versus criminals, religion versus the world, or security forces versus terrorists. The four pillars of cyber war must be mastered to engage effectively in those struggles.

In the summer of 2009 the National Resource Council, a think tank that has published several reports on cyber threats, produced a book titled: *Technology, Policy, Law, and Ethics Regarding U.S. Acquisition and Use of Cyberattack Capabilities.*

The NRC book is a comprehensive look at the question of engaging in cyberwar from the perspective of the United States. Its conclusion was that yes, the United States should acquire cyber attack capabilities.

This chapter identifies just how the United States, or any nation, would engage in cyberwar. By understanding these factors, the reader can gauge the threat to their own organization from cyberwar and perhaps take steps to prepare for either direct attacks or the fallout from an outbreak of cyber hostilities between nations.

INTELLIGENCE

According to the U.S. Army Field Manual 106 Information Operations, August 1996, the goal of cyberwar is "information dominance," defined as:

> The degree of information superiority that allows the possessor to use information systems and capabilities to achieve an operational advantage in a conflict or to control the situation in operations short of war, while denying those capabilities to the adversary.

But there is much more entailed in cyber warfare than that encapsulated in this simple definition. Intelligence-gathering as described throughout this book and, in particular, as practiced by the Chinese government and the People's Liberation Army can establish the type of information dominance that would provide an advantage during any widespread conflict. Effective intelligence-gathering provides a country with information that creates an advantage in many realms.

Political Intelligence-Gathering

By learning what your opponent is thinking, planning, and doing, an intelligence-gathering operation could provide critical information at an important juncture. Preparations for diplomatic engagements involve an understanding of the world situation and the points of view each party is bringing to a conference or treaty negotiation. Winston Churchill reports in *The Gathering Storm* the varied and fluid positions of Italy, Japan, the USSR, Poland, France, the UK, and Belgium during the lead-up to the declaration of war against Germany by Britain. There were many periods between 1933 and 1939 when World War II could have been avoided completely if a better understanding of each party's thinking were available. Hitler was engaged in a game of chess against the rest of the world. Even the German High Command thought he was risking too much as he ordered the Anschluss of Austria, the annexation of Czechoslovakia, and the invasion and partitioning of Poland. Hitler's actions, according to Churchill, were based on the true interpretation of France's and Britain's lack of desire to engage in all-out war. True up to his invasion of Poland, when Britain switched from pacifism to determination to prevail against all odds. But by then it was too late and world conflict had been initiated.

Weapons Intelligence

As the world powers turn from their historical aims of being able to fight protracted wars against one or two opposing countries to the recognition that fighting terrorists, rogue states, and groups dispersed throughout several countries, the weapons of war are changing. Cruise missiles, satellite-based weapons, remotely piloted drones, and rapidly deployed strike forces are areas of major investment for the United States and other world powers today. Gaining knowledge of planned weapons systems helps an adversary prepare weapons to counter the latest technology or even to copy that technology without the expense of research.

Military Intelligence

Knowledge of an adversary's military organization, the people in that organization, deployment numbers, disposition of resources, and state of preparedness are the domain of military intelligence. One of the most pivotal pieces of information ever gained through espionage (in fact from decrypting German High Command Communications) was that in the spring of 1944 Hitler held two complete divisions in reserve in the Netherlands. Knowing that Hitler's forces were not concentrated led the Allied Command to launch the D-Day landings at Normandy that subsequently led to the fall of the Third Reich and the complete victory of the Allies.

Industrial intelligence targets a company's or a country's manufacturing, banking, energy, and retail operations to glean information that could provide a boost to economic competitiveness. It could be as simple as stealing pricing data to help a competitor price their own products, or it could be stealing games, software, or video content for illegal reproduction. Despite the movement in recent years to a world economy that recognizes each country's contribution to global commerce, each nation-state still strives to grow and prosper in competition with the others. Industrial espionage is a tool of economic competition that is easily turned to enhancing a state's war-fighting capability.

An example of how information can benefit one party and harm the other can be found in the contract negotiations that Lee Iococca held with the United Auto Workers at a critical juncture for Chrysler as it struggled for survival in the late 1970s. A janitor, a union member who worked in the computer center at Chrysler, fished a green bar printout from the trash that contained the salaries of all of the executives and white-collar staff. This printout was famously taken to the negotiating table and thrown down in support of the union's position. Aside from harming management's position in union contract negotiations, that incident led to a revamping of security in Chrysler's computer operations. In particular, union members were barred from working in the data center!

The world has become digital since the late 1970s. Most information resides on computers. Most transmittal of information goes over networks, usually unencrypted. Most internal discussion of critical matters is recorded via electronic means and shared electronically and therefore is vulnerable to cyber espionage.

Recent examples of successful espionage are surely a small fraction of the number of instances of successful data theft. The U.S. military reports that the Chinese People's Liberation Army is now in possession of most of the design data for the Advanced Joint Strike Fighter designed and built at a cost of over $100 billion. A terabyte of data has been systematically culled from the so-called nonclassified NIPR net that ties together military contractors and government networks. (When the U.S. military announces a major loss of data they invariably state that no classified information was obtained by the spies. These statements are self-serving in that they are meant to highlight the need for better security [more funding] while protecting the jobs of those responsible for security. After all, if classified information were being stolen then courts-martial would be called for.)

The value of information transmitted across the unencrypted NIPR net is often minimized. Yet even encrypted network traffic can give an adversary critical information. There is a field of espionage called signal analysis. It is the practice of monitoring the source, direction, and length of transmissions to glean critical information. It was put to good use during World War II to monitor transmissions to and from German U-boats, and by the Germans to locate cargo convoys. In modern practice signal analysis can be applied to e-mail, Instant Messaging, VoIP (voice over Internet Protocol) calls, and file transfers. All IP packets have to contain a source and destination address, even if their payloads are encrypted with the strongest measures. By counting the volumes, frequency, and times of transmissions it is possible to determine much. If those transmissions are correlated with other activity it would be possible to determine things such as:

- Preparations for troop, aircraft, or ship deployments as transmission volume increases between a command center and an airfield or naval base.
- Participants in a particular military contract as the project center sends e-mails and files to defense contractors.
- Diplomatic activity as volume of traffic increases between the State Department and a consulate or embassy.
- In the event of a national emergency the volume of transmissions and the participants in those communications would reveal the inner workings of a government's response capabilities.

Thus, even so-called secure networks such as the U.S. military SIPRnet are subject to signal analysis and valuable information can be determined from the flow of encrypted data.

Countering cyber espionage takes a concerted effort that goes far beyond most organizations' current efforts to secure their cyber environments. (See chapter 3 for more on extending simple security maxims to create a protected environment.) Countering signal analysis goes a step further and means that the parties to critical transmissions have to take steps to obfuscate the timing and volume of their transmissions. One method, filling the communication pipe with a constant stream of encrypted data, would be an impractical solution. Too many such packed channels would add to the cost of maintaining those networks and clog the public networks.

One of the prime targets for the cyber spy is an e-mail server. Controlling an adversary's e-mail server gives the assailant the ability to copy all e-mails, block the sending of certain e-mails, and even to modify e-mails in transit. If cyber spies were to gain such control over the e-mail servers of the Pentagon, Whitehall (UK military command), and the German Chancellery, they would have a gold mine of information. And, in fact, each of these organizations has reported such incursions. The Pentagon claims they have spent the gargantuan sum of $100 million cleaning up after their e-mail servers were breeched by attacks apparently launched from source IP addresses owned by the Chinese People's Liberation Army. Germany and the UK have also publicly attributed the successful attacks on their e-mail servers to China. The GhostNet researchers uncovered that the office of the Dalai Lama had lost control of their e-mail server to Chinese operatives as well.

The effective use of cyber intelligence is therefore one of the four pillars of successful cyber warfare operations. There are three steps to creating and operating an effective cyber espionage capability: reconnaissance, acquisition, and analysis.

Cyber reconnaissance is the systematic discovery of target assets. Military command determines the types of information desired and the organizations to target. Let us for the moment name a new branch of the military or intelligence function: the cyber corps. The cyber corps carries on a continuous discovery of IT assets associated with each target. The targets may be the army, navy, air force, military command center, offices of the president, prime minister, chancellor, State Department, or Foreign Office. The assets to be discovered include DNS servers, web servers, e-mail servers, routers, firewalls, and databases. The reason reconnaissance requires continuous activity is that the assets are changing continuously. DNS servers are moved, web servers, databases, and networks are updated on a daily basis. Cyber reconnaissance is the practice of tracking all of those changes as well as the discovery of new assets as they are brought online or some change in network architectures exposes them. Reconnaissance would not be limited to external penetration activities but would include the input from in-situ spies and informants.

Acquisition is the execution of an attack against an identified target for the purpose of gathering the information it contains. Databases, web servers, and e-mail servers are ripe for such activities. Under concerted attack they yield their store of military plans, diplomatic correspondence, weapons design, and even economic data such as customer lists, prices, and financials. The actual movement of the discovered data is called exfiltration in military parlance.

Analysis of material discovered via cyber espionage is the most challenging task. Usually the information must be translated. Then it has to be interpreted, evaluated, turned into useful form, and finally delivered to the department or organization that can make best use of it: Industrial plans, designs, and processes sent to the internal industry; diplomatic content sent to State Department or Foreign Office; weapons and troop movements sent to the military.

Writing in the seminal 2004 work *On the Chinese Revolution in Military Affairs*, PLA Major General Li Bingyan states:

> In the information age there is information excess, information overload, information surplus, information inflation, and information overflow, and that is a new factor of war friction. One philosopher said that absolute light and absolute darkness have the same effect—we cannot see anything. With information overflow, the modern battle field is more richly colorful and an area for cunning and deception.[1]

Seeing the colors through the glare is the task of data analysis.

All three of these operations: reconnaissance, acquisition, and analysis are linked in that analysis of cyber intelligence may lead to the identification of new targets for reconnaissance, as may the acquisition activity. The cyber espionage operations are integrated with the larger intelligence community engaged in news analysis, psyops (psychological operations), and covert operations.

Cyber intelligence also contributes to the other three branches of an effective cyber war operation.

TECHNOLOGY

Every new form of war drives changes in technology. Conversely, as seen in chapter 12, the technology causes the change in the methods and outcomes of wars. Effective cyberwar is driven by the cyber equivalent of an arms race. The attacker discovers and devises new attack methodologies while the defender shores up his defenses by blocking ports, patching systems, and deploying technology. There are eleven areas of development in offensive technology to be brought to bear on the problems of cyberwar.

  1. *Vulnerability discovery and exploitation.* Every application on every server has what are called attack surfaces. These are program inputs and outputs that may be vulnerable to exploitation. The exploit could take advantage of a bug in the code that exposes its internal workings and accepts arbitrary commands that are passed through to the operating system, which in turn could give the attacker complete control of the target computer. The input vectors could come from network ports the application is listening on or user input from a web form or communication with another application. The attacker studies each application by looking at source code if it is available (as it is in all open source programs such as Firefox, Apache, or Joomla) or assembly code, which they access through a process called reverse engineering. An attacker can also pummel the application with randomly "fuzzed" input and watch for responses that indicate a previously undiscovered vulnerability has been exposed. An effective cyberwar operation would include a team whose sole purpose would be discovering such vulnerabilities and developing attack methodologies.

  Those attack methodologies should be designed to be easy to execute quickly and should be engineered so that the exploitation is hard to detect by the defender.

  In addition to new vulnerabilities most systems are replete with previously discovered vulnerabilities because they have not been patched or protected. A cyberwar operation would devise new ways to attack those systems by exploiting known vulnerabilities.

  2. *Automation is the best way to multiply the effectiveness of cyber attacks.* Once a specific IT asset has been identified an automated attack can open it up, search for and steal information, and then clean up its tracks. The defender may never know of the event. Completely automated attack solutions could scan for targets, identify them, exploit them, and retrieve data for later analysis.

  3. *Management of cyber warfare operations is in its infancy.* Most attacks are still orchestrated by one individual sitting at a computer. Managing the simultaneous attack against multiple targets using diverse tools, by many cyber operatives, and collecting the data or managing the control programs left behind after the attack is a capability that, when addressed by cyber warfare operations, will yield valuable results.

Cyber criminals have already made progress in managing their operations. Phishing attacks involve copying the look of a target system, usually a bank but potentially any application that has user access controls, spamming millions of e-mail accounts, and finally recording user access credentials and breaking into accounts and transferring funds out of them. Today there are management consoles that can be installed on a compromised machine that provide a web interface to the entire phishing operation, including storing the identities of compromised accounts. That level of automation and central management will soon be practiced by cyber warriors.

4. Malware. Some discovered exploits lend themselves to the writing of software packages that can take advantage of vulnerabilities to install themselves on the target system. This is the realm of viruses, worms, and Trojan horses. A cyber warfare operation would employ teams whose responsibility it was to create such malware. The purposes would be multifold.

Viruses and worms can be used to recruit vulnerable machines into a botnet. This is no more than a collection of compromised computers that listen and respond to commands. Those commands could be instructions to download new components, which could in turn launch denial of service attacks, sniff and report network traffic, or eavesdrop on e-mail, IM, and web conversations.

The spread of malware can also have the effect of a widely cast net. The attacker hopes that by sifting through the results of reports from thousands, even millions, of infected machines he may identify a machine belonging to a key member of a target organization. It is hypothesized that this is the manner in which a significant chunk of source code for the Windows OS was stolen. A computer belonging to a Microsoft developer who worked from home was infected. His remote access (VPN) credentials were stolen, and the Windows source code eventually ended up on the Internet as the object of an auction.

Trojan horses are a primary technology of cyber warfare. A Trojan horse is code that is surreptitiously installed on a computer and grants the attacker remote control over his target. The defense against them that is most widely deployed is signature-based anti-virus software. It is very easy for an attacker to write new code or customize existing code so that it is not detectable by AV programs because they have no signature for something that the AV researchers have never seen before.

Refer back to the Haephrati Trojan fiasco in Israel. Private investigators in Israel used malware customized by Michael Haephrati to steal data from competitors of their industrial espionage clients. The GhostNet researchers discovered that China was using similar methods against the Dalai Lama's operations.

Cyberwar operations should be constantly evolving such tools to enhance the ease with which they can be installed on a target machine, the ability to avoid detection, and the ability to create unnoticed connections back to a data-collecting server. Cyber defense operations have to concern themselves with detecting and rendering harmless such Trojan horses.

5. Rootkits are a special form of malware. They attack the kernel of an operating system and can work "under the wire" at a lower level than defensive measures such as AV software, so they are undetectable even from a careful examination of the computer. Rootkits could be distributed as part of a commercial application. A cyberwar effort could even enlist the producers of commercial software that would be sold to targets.

6. Backdoors. The inclusion of spyware or hardware backdoors in products shipped to an enemy is a powerful way to wage cyberwar. Accusations of such activity are usually no more than paranoia. To date. It is maintained by many that printers shipped to Iraq before the first Gulf War contained backdoors that allowed the U.S. to access Iraqi command and control networks in advance of the invasion. Most vendors of IT products address a global market and would not readily jeopardize their sales by acquiescing to the inclusion of backdoors in their products because of the harm to their reputation if they are uncovered. But the development and deployment of such tools in an enemy's environment is a valuable goal and would be pursued by any cyberwar effort.

One scheme has been proposed that a nation, particularly the United States, could in times of extreme need induce their software industry to push updates to their installed base that included malware that could be used to disable their enemy's computers. Imagine the impact Microsoft, Cisco, or Oracle could have if they used their automatic update capability to secretly infect millions of machines with back doors, Trojan horses, or kill switches.

7. Analysis. If ever there was a task for business intelligence (BI) solutions, the evaluation and reduction of the terabytes of data collected from cyber espionage activities is it. Technologies developed for this analysis will be a critical factor in the escalation of cyber capabilities. Signal analysis, mentioned above, is just one such task. Others include:

Tracking sources and the information derived from them. A database of military personnel including their ranks, specialties, training, commendations, and deployments would be updated continuously. Tracking those changes and their significance would be a difficult task without assistance from data analysis tools.

Correlating information derived from different sources or dates. A missile design, for instance, goes through hundreds of revisions for each component as dimensions, materials, and manufacturing processes are optimized throughout the life-cycle of a design. An attacker may have different copies of CAD models, process sheets, and engineering specifications that vary with time, model, and manufacturer. Determining which was the best design or which reflected the current state of the missile in question would require sophisticated BI tools.

The acquisition of a single e-mail between two parties does not represent their entire conversation on a topic. Any correspondence may contain errors or be updated by a follow-on e-mail. Pulling together the entire thread of a conversation is a challenge even for the participants!

If the goal of cyberwar is total information dominance, the generals would want to know the economic, military, supply, staffing, and technological standing of their advisaries who are engaged in collaboration, and mutual defense accords. Only by developing powerful and automated analytical capabilities will modern-day generals be able to conduct cyberwar.

8. DDoS technology. As covered extensively in chapter 7, denial of service can take many forms. Developing new methods of attacking routers, servers, and switches via specially crafted packets or floods of packets are critical areas of technology development for cyber warfighting capability.

9. Compromising routing infrastructure via BGP route announcements is another weapon of cyberwar. Planning how to achieve the desired results of shutting off an adversary while maintaining network functionality for the attacker is an area of technology to be investigated.

10. DNS attacks. By controlling DNS servers or simply making them inaccessible, an attacker can gain the upper hand in a cyber conflict. If Georgia's attackers in 2008 had simply owned the DNS server for the .ga Top Level Domain they could have simply pointed all traffic to alternative sites with their own messages instead of the intended destination.

11. SCADA attacks. SCADA is a protocol used specifically for sending commands to and receiving data from the switches and pumps that control power grids and oil and gas pipelines. Developing the tools to attack these networks that control critical infrastructure would be a primary technology advantage in cyberwar.

Farewell Dossier and U.S. Targeted Attack against the Soviet Union

Thomas C. Reed, former secretary of the U.S. Air Force, and member of Reagan's National Security Council relates a magnificent story in *At the Abyss: An Insider's History of the Cold War*. He draws on recently published notes of Dr. Gus Weiss, NSC member in Reagan's first term. Reagan had been told of a KGB agent who had been turned by France into a double agent in a summit meeting with French President Mitterrand in Ottawa. This agent, code named, in a preminiscent coincidence, Farewell, had revealed a massive Soviet espionage apparatus that was actively collecting intelligence from U.S. military and industrial organizations. Colonel Vladimir I. Vetrov, the Farewell agent, provided details of the Soviet's infiltration of U.S. laboratories, factories, and government agencies. As Reed points out, the arms race between the two countries was being led by the United States with the Soviet Union right behind as they engaged in well-coordinated intelligence-gathering involving hundreds of case officers, agents in place, and informants. Even one of the Soviet Cosmonauts delegated to the Apollo-Soyuz joint space mission was a KGB agent.

The information gleaned from agent Farewell provided an understanding of the Soviet shopping list for technology that proved key to the U.S. response. Under the direction of Dr. Weiss, the United States began to systematically poison the information that the KGB gathered. "Extra ingredients" in the form of buggy software and Trojan horses were added to the software and components that these agents acquired. "Pseudosoftware disrupted factory output. Flawed but convincing ideas on stealth, attack aircraft, and space defense made their way into Soviet ministries."[2]

The penultimate example that Weiss reveals in his notes shows how the placement of a ticking time bomb in control software was used to disrupt the lifeblood of the Soviet economy: oil and gas distribution. It is a lesson those responsible for critical infrastructure protection should take to heart. A KGB agent penetrated a Canadian control software vendor. Learning of this, the United States planted control software at the vendor that contained a Trojan horse, a ticking time bomb. The buggy software was deployed throughout the Soviet Union's pipeline control system. The software running the pumps, valves, and turbines was set to disrupt those operations at a future time, when pump speeds, and valve settings would cause pressure fluctuations that would destroy the pipeline. The ensuing explosion was recorded by U.S. spy satellites. What appeared to be a three kiloton explosion from space was in fact the result of a software time bomb.

The economic disruption from the loss of a major pipeline was one result of this purported cyber attack. Another effect was that, as the Soviets came to understand what had happened, they lost faith in all of their software and controls as well as other intelligence they had been relying on. When the United States and NATO rolled up the Soviet spy ring in 1984–85 the Soviet Union became blind to further U.S. technological advancement. They were in the dark about the progress of the Strategic Defense Initiative (Star Wars) and had lost faith in their earlier intelligence gathered from a now disrupted source.

The lesson to be learned is that cyber warfare techniques were used successfully in the early 1980s. The military leaders of the world are now fully aware of the damage that can be done by the surreptitious introduction of bugged code. Now that the Internet, which was in its infancy in 1982, has connected critical systems to a global network, the possibilities for exploitation are much greater. Cyberwar methodologies focused on similar types of disruption—economic, physical, and psychological, must be developed to achieve "information dominance."

LOGISTICS

Without supply chains and the efficient flow of weapons, reserves, fuel, and food a war cannot be waged effectively, if at all. In the cyber realm logistics takes a different path than in the real world. Rather than treating the science and issues of delivering a strike force to a theater of war and supplying them in such a way that they can continue to operate, cyber logistics deals with networks and the ability to deliver an attack while also defending those network paths that attacks would come across. Cyber logistics treats with the availability of network paths. This could be the direct network connection between a particular facility and the Internet or the major fiber paths that connect a country. Estonia is served by two sea fiber cables and one overland fiber connection through Lithuania. Georgia found itself vulnerable to isolation because it had limited connectivity to the rest of world, some of it easily controlled by their Russian adversary.

Control and defense of routers that manage Internet connectivity is critical to both cyber defense and offense. Hardening those routers from attack and making sure that they communicate only with trusted sources of route announcements is critical to maintaining cyber logistics. A malicious route announcement, as demonstrated in the now famous instance of Pakistan and YouTube (see chapter 7), could completely disable a military or commercial operation's ability to communicate over the Internet. In the Pakistan case an engineer accidently uploaded a BGP instruction to his main router that was picked up by the trusting routers of his upstream provider and thence to the rest of the world. A malicious attack would be as simple and effective. An aggressor could announce that google.com resided in a target's network, simultaneously causing a DDoS on that target as billions of requests for Google were routed to it and seriously interrupting Google's availability. Physical attacks against fiber especially at major Internet exchanges could pose a serious threat and conversely should be part of any plans for complete information dominance as practiced in cyber warfare.

The Domain Name Service (DNS) is a critical component of cyber logistics. Without DNS it is impossible to resolve a particular web URL into its underlying IP address. An attack on the DNS is as effective as attacking the primary target.

At a higher level there are common communications channels that are becoming more and more important. The community of blogs and news sites is interconnected via RSS feeds (Real Simple Syndication, a protocol/service that allows articles to be reposted, aggregated, even e-mailed). Social sites such as Twitter and Facebook are a primary means of disseminating information quickly if not necessarily accurately.

Twitter interfaces with phone systems via SMS text messages. An attack on Twitter, Facebook, and the popular blogging site Live Journal in July of 2009 caused a disruption to many people's means of communication (see chapter 11).

Effective cyber defense would include the creation of alternative networks to act as ready standbys in the event of a successful attack. It would be possible to route traffic over analog lines if needed or via radio, microwave, and satellite links. The alternative networks would be hardened against multiple vectors perhaps even including EMP (Electro Magnetic Pulse) from an upper atmosphere detonation of a nuclear device. EMP has been identified as the single most vulnerable aspect of most industrialized nations. The detonation of a small nuclear device in the upper atmosphere causes a huge shock wave of electrical energy that is picked up by every electronic device in the line of sight, which from that high up is a considerable distance. Power transmission lines, transformers, generators, every modern automobile, every cell phone, router, server, and computer would be destroyed. It could take from six months to a year for a region to recover from such an attack.

Hardening a country's critical infrastructure, power, oil and gas lines, emergency communications against EMP involves shielding every transmission line, pumping station, and telephone switch; an investment that has been made in only the most critical installations. The world's nations have focused on nuclear arms control as its main defense against EMP.

COMMAND AND CONTROL

Technology developments in command and control are important adjuncts to the issue of connectivity and the fourth pillar of cyber warfare. One of the primary targets of cyberwar is the communication infrastructure by which a defending army conducts its response to an outbreak of hostilities. During the Russian attacks against Georgia in August 2008 one of the most important tools the president of Georgia (a minuscule state compared to Russia) had was his ability to broadcast the situation to a world otherwise occupied with the Summer Olympics in Beijing. He used his website to do so. The Russian attacks against websites of the Georgian state served to quiet his cry of protest while Russian tanks poured across the border into the Georgian district of South Ossetia.

Communicating secretly, reliably, and without tampering is a key to waging war. Disrupting command and control is a primary goal of cyberwar in support of a full-scale war. Developing the capability to defend command and control channels from cyber attack should be a focus of the cyber preparedness of any nation or, for that matter, any organization that expects to be under cyber attack. Developing cyber attack methodologies that target an adversary's command and control infrastructure is a key element of cyberwar capabilities.

Understanding these four pillars is important for most organizations. Any business, local government, or even individuals that rely on the Internet and computing resources for efficient operations should study the methods of cyber warfare if they want to gain an understanding of the new threat level extant today. Countering those threats, as spelled out in previous chapters, will become a bigger part of their Information Technology budgets as well as their business risk assessments.

Mastering the four pillars of cyberwar as defined in this chapter is of paramount importance to any nation that expects to engage in and survive future wars. But to do so those nations must also change the organization of their current military and the way in which it is guided by General HQ and ultimately the state leaders. Just how should that be done? In the next chapter we address the changes in the way nations are addressing the looming threat of cyber war. Estonia has taken a simple, effective path. The United States, from the White House down to the newly formed Air Force Cyber Command in San Antonio, Texas, is facing major upheavals.

CYBER PREPAREDNESS

This chapter discusses the efforts under way to prepare for cyberwar on the part of the United States and other nations. Estonia's home guard is contrasted with the massive changes within the United States and its creation of CYBERCOM. Other nations are following the leads of these two countries to varying degrees.

> *Still, if you will not fight for the right when you can easily win without bloodshed, if you will not fight when your victory will be sure and not so costly, you may come to the moment when you will have to fight with all the odds against you and only a precarious chance for survival. There may be a worse case. You may have to fight when there is no chance of victory, because it is better to perish than to live as slaves.*
>
> —Winston Churchill, *The Gathering Storm*

Just how well have the United States and other countries prepared for waging war in a cyber world? Unfortunately the nonaggressor states are repeating a pattern that has prevailed throughout military history. They are slow to recognize the need for preparedness and do not devote the necessary resources to fight the next war. Pacifist states that are ultimately victorious rely, perhaps rightly, on their ability to ramp up a response when needed.

In June 1935, over 11 million people in Britain signed a petition calling for a reduction in armaments by international treaty. That was only four years before Hitler ignited World War II on September 1, 1939. The isolationist United States was even slower to respond to the combined threat of Japan and Germany on two widely separated fronts. Yet, in both World War I and World War II the defenders ultimately devoted their entire economy and the lives of their populace to pursue victory.

While this chapter shows the United States, Britain, and other nations to be slow to respond to the threat of cyberwar, and their leaders and generals perhaps not equipped to deal with the technological challenges, the cost and threat to privacy that converting to a cyberwar footing would entail may explain that lethargy. The pacifist states once again find themselves bound by their democratic processes and at a disadvantage compared to more dictatorial aggressors.

To an IT security professional the governments of the world appear to be reacting far too slowly to the rise of cyber threats. Yet, there is now a flurry of activity; perhaps more organizational than concrete. This chapter addresses the ramp-up of cyber preparedness throughout the governments of the world. First we discuss the United States, which has the largest and slowest ship to turn. Then Estonia, a nimble, almost newborn country that has suffered direct cyber attack and has responded. Ireland, the UK, Germany, India, Pakistan, and Israel also have active cyber programs. China's cyber capabilities have been addressed in earlier chapters, as has what is visible of Russia's activities.

THE UNITED STATES

On May 29, 2009, President Barack Obama gave the first cogent public address on cyber security by a U.S. leader: "Protecting this infrastructure will be a national security priority. We will ensure that these networks are secure, trustworthy, and resilient," Obama said. "We will deter, prevent, detect, and defend against attacks and recover quickly from any disruptions or damage."[1]

But the United States has actually been gaining in its understanding of cyber threats for several years as the evidence mounted that military and research facilities were under attack from adversaries. The acknowledgment of Titan Rain and the activities of Shawn Carpenter heralded the beginnings of a serious response to cyber threats. The attacks on the Pentagon that led to a major investment in reshaping the IT infrastructure at the core of the U.S. Armed Forces, the attacks against military theater operations spread via USB memory sticks, and repeated DDoS attacks against U.S. government websites have led the United States to get serious; first about cyber defense, second to acquire cyber offense capabilities.

Comprehensive National Cybersecurity Initiative

On January 8, 2008, the Bush administration issued directives creating the Comprehensive National Cybersecurity Initiative (CNCI). While the actual substance of the initiative remains classified, details have emerged from National Security Presidential Directive 54/Homeland Security Presidential Directive 23 that enumerate its 12 components:

1. Trusted Internet Connections (TIC). This project predates Directive 54/23 and is well under way. It is based on the idea that it is easier to defend a smaller perimeter. Federal networks grew organically over the decades since TCP/IP networks including the Internet came to be. Little thought was given to security because there were few known threats over those years. Now the government is struggling to contain the haphazard growth of network connections.

As of June 4, 2008, the status of TIC was:

CURRENT AND TARGET CONNECTIONS
(AGENCY REPORTED)
Existing Connections (Jan 2008) = 4300+
Existing Connections (May 2008) = 2758
   Target Connections <100[2]

Achieving that target of less than 100 network gateways would make the task of securing the U.S. government networks much simpler.

2. IDS (Intrusion Detection Systems). This project, code-named Einstein II, is the responsibility of the United States Computer Emergency

Readiness Team. (Note that US-CERT changed the traditional translation of the acronym to "Readiness" from "Response"; a subtle rebranding.) Once they have reduced the number of Internet connections, the plan is to deploy IDS at each one of them to monitor intrusions. Monitoring intrusions has a defeatist sound to it. It appears to acknowledge that the networks will be attacked successfully and that data-gathering technology will only provide evidence after the fact of those intrusions. When Clifford Stoll wrote *The Cuckoo's Egg*, it was an exciting idea to track down intruders via telltale signatures of their activity. Shawn Carpenter's role at Sandia and Lockheed Martin was to review IDS logs. The repercussions of what he found, if taken to heart, would lead to more protective deployments of technology. Today, those Internet connections see millions of attempted attacks. The resources it would take to analyze and react to each attack would be better spent on making those networks more secure. One can see how the U.S. government could be interested in collecting all that data and assigning the people and resources to analyzing it. They could derive useful information from pattern and trend analysis.

3. IPS (Intrusion Prevention System). This project has the code name Einstein III. Not only would it identify the attacks in real time, but ideally it would block them. Most businesses around the world already have deployed some types of IPS. In 2008 then secretary of the Department of Homeland Security (DHS) Michael Chertoff said he'd like to see a government computer infrastructure that could look for early indications of computer skullduggery and stop it before it happens.

The system "would literally, like an anti-aircraft weapon, shoot down an attack before it hits its target," he said. "And that's what we call Einstein 3.0."[3]

4. R&D coordination. Review the projects at all of the government research labs and make sure they are working together. Since the days of Shawn Carpenter at Sandia, the U.S. research labs have launched numerous projects to develop cyber security technology. This provision of CNCI would attempt to corral that activity into a manageable whole.

5. Connecting centers of expertise such as US-CERT. As observed in Estonia, getting those responsible for networks and critical servers to communicate in time of crisis is the most concrete preparation for cyberwar.

6. TOP SECRET. The sixth element of CNCI is classified. It probably deals with cyber espionage.

7. Counterintelligence. Identifying, monitoring, and shutting down the activities of cyber spies, and presumably working with myriad U.S. intelligence groups (over 18 according to www.intelligence.gov/ 1-members.shtml).

8. Education and workforce training. DHS is very concerned that they do not have enough qualified workers to implement their programs. They are engaged in active hiring and training. A report in 2009 stated they were hiring 1,000 new employees for cyber security purposes.

9. Leap ahead technologies. As nothing has been published it is hard to tell the types of activity this may entail. Certainly vulnerability discovery, host hardening, and network defenses would be part of any investment in new technology.

10. Deterrence. As in nuclear deterrence. This is the idea that you would threaten potential attackers with the idea that the United States will attack back. Of course, a few tactically placed charges of high explosive (HE) on undersea cables able to be set off with a remote command might be effective deterrence. Other means of deterrence are problematic. Most attacks to date have been almost impossible to attribute to a particular group, let alone a country. How can you deter an unknown assailant?

11. Supply chain risk management. This could address several disparate factors. Many computer and network components are manufactured overseas. That represents a risk. The UK intelligence community has expressed concern over British Telecom's, for instance, using network gear provided by Huawei, a Chinese company founded by a member of the People's Liberation Army.

12. Critical infrastructure protection. This is called Project 12 within the beltway. It involves a lot of public-private partnership and appears to be the main responsibility of the Director of Critical Infrastructure Cyber Protection and Awareness, National Cyber Security Division, U.S. Department of Homeland Security. This could include:

- Bidirectional information-sharing between government and industry.
- Incentives. Ways to encourage security through some sort of reward for better security that offsets the cost.
- Sharing federal capabilities.

- R&D coordination. See #4 above.
- Share classified information with service providers who are the most forward deployed networks.

Early in his term President Obama called on one of the government contractors who had helped the Bush administration to draft the CNCI to review it and make a proposal. On May 29, he announced the result: Melissa Hathaway returned a short document that was rebranded to the Cyberspace Policy Review (CPR). Its primary suggestion was the creation of an office of cyber security policy review and the appointment of a cyber security policy coordinator (Howard Schmidt), who would work with the various branches of the government, military, and intelligence agencies to coordinate policy. But this person would not set or enforce policies.

Despite slow movement from the executive branch, the U.S. military has moved ahead with cyberwar preparations. These include:

The creation of a Cyber Command under the Strategic Command (STRATCOM) led by the head of the National Security Agency (NSA, the U.S. intelligence agency), Lieutenant General Keith Alexander, who will have both roles (USCYBERCOM and NSA). The cyber units associated with each branch of the military will be under his operational control. These include the U.S. Army, U.S. Navy, U.S. Marine Corps, and U.S. Air Force cyber commands as well as supporting other combat commanders.

The Cyber Command will support the director of the Defense Information Systems Agency (DISA), which in turn has input into a joint operations center that will be the core of operations under the command of a deputy cyber commander.

CYBERCOM officially "stood up" in October 2009. It was predated slightly by the U.S. Air Force's creation of the Air Force Cyber Command based at Lackland Air Force Base outside San Antonio, Texas, August 18, 2009.

The newly designated 24th Air Force staff will provide combat-ready forces trained and equipped to conduct sustained cyber operations, integrated within air and space operations. The Air Force 688th Information Operations Center and the 67th Network Warfare Wing were combined under the new 24th Air Force.[4]

On October 1, 2009, the U.S. Navy announced the creation of an "Information Dominance Corps" within the Fleet Cyber Command that would include 44,000 personnel and that 1,000 new cyber warriors would be hired or trained. That many personnel represent all of the navy's intelligence, computer, and information operations staff, combined to take advantage of the new awareness of cyberspace as a war-fighting domain. The organization is aligned with the Cyber Command. Note that the new title reflects the U.S. military's stated goal of "Information Dominance." The leader of this new corps bears the title: Director of Information Dominance.[5]

The U.S. Army has yet to announce an overarching cyber command. Their significant Information Operations (IO) and Network War Fighting capabilities are being coordinated by the the 1st Information Operations Command (IOC), which works with (but does not command) the army personnel working with Joint Task Force–Global Network Operations. IOC also works with the National Security Agency (NSA), and Joint Functional Component Command–Network Warfare, Army Network Operations (NetOps) forces assigned to the Army Network Enterprise Technology Command/9th Signal Command, as well as Network Warfare (NetWar) forces assigned to the Army Intelligence and Security Command (INSCOM). With computer, network, and information resources disbursed throughout a military command, the need for centralization is having a real impact on the organization of the U.S. military.

In September 2009, the U.S. Marine Corps published a position paper indicating they are preparing their own response to the challenge of cyberwar operations. The paper states that the U.S. Marine Corps

> needs to take full advantage of potential offensive opportunities in the cyberspace domain and to minimize the asymmetric, critical vulnerabilities created by our reliance on networked communications. The Marine Corps should develop a comprehensive understanding and approach to cyberspace operations that fully integrate all aspects of computer network operations, information assurance, and network operations under a single command or proponent.[6]

Outside the military, the National Cybersecurity Division (NCSD) within the U.S. Department of Homeland Security bears responsibility for overall cyber security in the United States. It oversees US-CERT and coordinates activities between public and commercial security groups as part of their mandate. In addition, DHS operates the Office of Cybersecurity and Communications, which is concerned with protecting critical information infrastructure. One more organization, the National Cyber Security Center, is a very small office. Its first head, Rod

Beckstrom, resigned after its first year amid the confusion at DHS and the White House over how to centrally coordinate the many organizations within the federal government that deal with cyber security. It is still unclear how these DHS and White House cyber security offices will work with the DoD Cyber Command.

ESTONIA

Estonia has a total population (1.4 million), almost exactly the same as the number of active duty personnel in the U.S. military. Yet Estonia has taken steps to reflect the new reality of cyber preparedness in the aftermath of the Russian cyber attacks of April 2007 (as reported in chapter 9).

In 2006 Estonia staffed the Cooperative Cyber Defence Centre of Excellence (CCDCOE), a NATO-sponsored research and development team, on the outskirts of the capital of Tallinn. That team provided the first analysis of the April attacks in 2007. The Centre became fully operational in August 2008. They also helped deploy cyber advisors to Georgia when that country underwent similar attacks in August 2008. The Estonian Ministry of Defense is not directly involved in the operations of the CCDCOE, but contributed resources to its establishment, including personnel.

According to Heli Tiirmaa-Klaa, within the Ministry of Defense, Estonia recognizes that control of networks and critical infrastructure does not actually reside within the government, so they have worked to improve the readiness of the country by making sure that key personnel from their banks, ISPs, and government IT staff are in communication and able to react quickly, just as they did in an ad hoc manner in April 2007. High-level government officials must take cyber security training and awareness classes. This simple understanding of the real and present danger and the measured response capability is refreshing compared to the massive reorganizations that are occurring throughout the military establishments of most major powers.

THE UNITED KINGDOM

In June 2009 the United Kingdom published its Cyber Security Strategy, which outlined the creation of an Office of Cyber Security (OCS) to provide strategic leadership for the government, and a Cyber Security Operations Centre (CSOC) to monitor and respond to cyber activity. The CSOC is to be colocated with GCHQ's Cheltenham Headquarters. GCHQ is one of the three UK intelligence agencies (along with the more famous MI5 and MI6). This association between cyber defense and existing intelligence organizations mirrors the United States' making the head of the NSA the head of USCYBERCOM.

The UK has also funded a new research and development center in Northern Ireland called the Centre for Secure Information Technologies (CSIT), based at Queen's University Belfast. It is backed with about $50 million to research technologies to fight viruses, analyze CCTV data from the thousands of cameras the government has deployed around its cities, and improve security processors (the chips used in routers and firewalls) to identify and block attacks.

EUROPE

At a meeting of the European Union (EU) Ministries for Critical Information Infrastructure Protection held in Tallinn, Estonia, in April 2009, much of the discussion focused on the creation of Computer Emergency Response Teams. This focus on CERTs is interesting. The idea is that those who are in the best position to react to cyber attacks get to know each other, share contact details, and meet every quarter to build up trust. As most of the people who can actually be effective during attacks are network and security geeks, it is not always an easy task to get their employers to let them participate. These are the guys who keep the wheels on the bus turning. Allowing them to attend meetings in warm places that serve good mojitos (a favorite libation of security geeks) is not exactly what makes telecom and government organizations happy.

CERTs, in practice, reflect the reality of how cyber emergencies are handled. Someone notices something strange going on, a packet flood, a downed network, inability to get to YouTube or Gmail, and he uses whatever channel is available to contact other security community members to ask what they see from their positions on the network. He may join a discussion in IRC (a chat room). He usually figures out what is happening, determines a response, and passes it to someone who addresses the issue. That person might correct some routing tables, change DNS for a domain, or get on the phone to an ISP to get them to block traffic from an offending server. So formalizing the connections between those who run the Internet is a good idea. At the time of publishing there were 128 CERTs in Europe. The European Network of Information Security (ENISA) is an EU agency that attempts to coordinate the activities of EU member state CERTs. In the way of large government bureaucracies the world over, it was set up in out-of-the-way Crete. Its effectiveness has been criticized in part because each nation-state tends to want to keep their key cyber security players at home and they tend to not share as well as they might.

Aside from the military organizations in each country, the members of NATO are investing in their own cyber defense capabilities. NATO created the Cyber Defence Management Authority (CDMA) in Brussels to provide operational assistance if and when a member state is under attack. The impetus for setting up the CDMA was the attack against Estonia, which is often credited with sending a "wake-up call" to Europe.

GERMANY

Germany's cyber defenses are under the command of a brigadier general, Friedrich Wilhelm Kriesel, who heads an Air Force division called Bundeswehr's Strategic Reconnaissance Unit, a 6,000-strong intelligence operation. The cyber department in the Tomburg barracks in Rheinbach is called the Department of Information and Computer Network Operations.

RUSSIA

Apparently Russia, often cited as the instigator of attacks, has not formalized its cyberwar organization. There are few official statements of their preparations for or use of cyber capabilities in war. The Russian Information Security Doctrine approved by Putin in September 2000 is out of date and does not address cyberwar or preparedness. Speaking at a conference at the U.S. National Defense University in April 2009, Alexey A. Salnikov, vice director of Russia's Information Security Institute, voiced concerns about cyber attacks used in state conflicts, indicating that Russia is aware of the potential for cyberwar but not addressing any steps it has taken to prepare for cyberwar

SOUTH KOREA

In the aftermath of the July attacks on 39 sites belonging to South Korea and the United States, South Korea announced at the end of November 2009 that it would create a new Cyber Defense Command under the Ministry of Defense's intelligence headquarters, the group that already engages in monitoring North Korean communications via radio listening posts and gathering other intelligence. The new Cyber Defense Command will be under the charge of a major general and by the time it is fully operational in 2012 will employ 400–500 cyber warriors.

NORTH KOREA

While there is much speculation that attributes a huge cyber army to North Korea there is not much evidence. It appears that North Korea does have an official cyber unit in the general political bureau of the Ministry of the People's Armed Forces.

AUSTRALIA

Australia announced in November 2009 that the government was creating a new Computer Emergency Response Team. This CERT-Australia would take over the current operations of the existing GOV-CERT, supplementing and sometimes supporting the already private AUS-CERT.

FRANCE

In July 2009, France announced the formation of the French Networks and Information Security Agency (FNSI). The new agency is tasked with monitoring sensitive French networks and information operations; it employs 150 people. It supersedes the Central Information Systems Security Division, which had been created in 2001. FNSI reports to the prime minister and is under the general secretary for national defense.[7]

The world is still refocusing government approaches to security and recognizing the military implications of network-attached resources that are vulnerable to cyber attacks. Cyberwar fighting is being studied in the United States and China and presumably in Russia. The implications are that more spending, more organizational changes, and more incidents are on the horizon. The next chapter delves into the repercussions of these changes.

REPERCUSSIONS

Approaching apocalypse? No. Yet the advent of cyberwar is already wreaking change. This chapter predicts what cyberwar means for the future of the Internet and its geopolitical implications.

A democracy which makes or even effectively prepares for modern, scientific war must necessarily cease to be democratic. No country can be really well prepared for modern war unless it is governed by a tyrant, at the head of a highly trained and perfectly obedient bureaucracy.

—Aldous Huxley

Just what does the rise of cyber warfare mean for business, governments, technology, and the Internet? The rapidly changing technological universe is bound to impact every aspect of human endeavor. Steam power, the telegraph, internal combustion engines, and the nuclear age have all pushed the human race forward while introducing new threats to safety, the stability of governments, and democratic freedoms. The changes in communication and commerce wrought by the Internet are still having repercussions that were unpredicted at its inception. The impact of a global network that ties together all people who have achieved a certain level of technology and literacy is proving to be as disruptive as every other shift in technology and community in our history.

History is filled with examples of well-intentioned endeavors that ultimately become the targets of greed and crime and the Internet is no different. As each wave of early adaptors rushed to access the Internet, it should have been easy to predict the rise of cybercrime. Spam, unsolicited advertising, was the first sign that unsavory elements had discovered that there was money to be made by a universal, almost anonymous connection to millions of people. An early community on the Internet, Network News, made it possible for participants to self-organize by interests. There were newsgroups for everything: hedgehog lovers, knitters, movie enthusiasts, and politicos. After the first spam message was posted by two attorneys in Florida hawking their immigration services, thousands of copycat spammers flooded the newsgroups with their messages. When AOL first hooked up its million-strong community of subscribers to the Internet in 1995 it exposed a huge number of people to unscrupulous spammers and hackers that would prey on the neophytes entering this brave new world.

E-mail was the next protocol to succumb to spam. Addresses culled from news groups and naïve users who posted their e-mail addresses on the World Wide Web were used to spread marketing messages for software, Viagra, and pornography. Network news groups soon died under the onslaught of spam. But e-mail was too important to lose, and the need for defenses against spam fueled a multibillion-dollar industry.

Spammers crossed the line from the questionable to the criminal when they began to use adware. They would induce the unwary to download screen savers, weather tool bars, and flapping butterfly cursors. Buried in the download would be Trojan horses that would redirect their search results to paid search sites, pop up ads, and sometimes even record keystrokes and passwords, giving the attacker access to their bank accounts.

As more of the world became networked, the types of criminal uses blossomed. Nigerian advanced-fee scammers who had previously used postal mail discovered how rich they could become using the free and easy Internet. Russian organized crime syndicates discovered that they could use botnets to fuel their carding operations with stolen credit cards from banking databases.

Because of natural lethargy and perceived costs, several sectors have been slow to get online or completely leverage the Internet. Banks were slow to recognize the benefit of interacting with their customers via the Web. Their primary reservation, however, was not security risks, but the costs. When U.S. banks finally embraced the Internet their naïveté created a risk model that had them writing off losses instead of investing to prevent them. One significant repercussion that derives directly from this lack of investment is the financing of cyber criminal activities. By indemnifying their retail users from any loss associated with the online use of credit cards or bank accounts, banks were essentially encouraging credit card theft and unauthorized account access. The illicit gains of the cyber criminals encouraged others to join their ranks. As millions of credit cards enter the black market, bigger and bigger targets are sought, using increasingly sophisticated attack methodologies.

The banks, in part, created their enemy through lack of defense. Now cyber criminals engage in elaborate schemes that involve hundreds of players—one team creates phishing campaigns to steal accounts, another team manufactures ATM cards, and field operatives withdraw funds from dozens of ATMs simultaneously. Other schemes involve breaking into online stock trading accounts, liquidating the owner's holdings, and buying penny stocks that the attacker has invested in. When the surge in activity pumps the stock price up, the cyber criminal dumps it. When it crashes, the account holder is left with nothing.

The Internet has a way of penetrating all walks of life, businesses, and even governments, despite efforts by their IT departments. These organizations have no plans for adopting new technology, and certainly no strategy for securing their operations as ad hoc deployments promulgate throughout their sector. A well-meaning IT staff member or even end user might publish internal documents online, connect internal networks to the Internet, even enable SMS controls of their critical servers and routers to make his job easier, with unintended results. WiFi deployments in remote offices, bank branches, manufacturing plants, even power and pumping stations open those networks to drive-by attackers equipped with laptops.

What we are now experiencing is the discovery of the war-fighting possibilities of the Internet, as terrorist groups, religious factions, and aggressor states realize the great potential for doing harm empowered by the Internet.

The news is full of predictions of impending cyber calamity. Some with vested interests in security companies, or increased budgets, cry "Cybergeddon," "Cyber apocalypse," and even "Cyber Katrina!" But the world has already experienced cyber warfare as described in this book. There is no need to paint pictures of impending doom to justify further investment in cyber defense. That expense is clearly justified.

Cyber espionage is already with us. Although loss of life or regime change resulting from cyber warfare is possible, communities and countries have survived disasters that are much greater.

But there are repercussions to the rise of cyber attacks. Repercussions that will drive technology development, security software and hardware, and the adoption of safe practices for conducting business online. Some of these will entail restrictions on the free and easy use of the Internet. Some of these will change how governments operate. And some will impact the world's military organizations and the way they conduct their operations and engage with their enemies.

IMPACT ON MILITARY ORGANIZATIONS

As we saw in the previous chapter, the militaries of the world are recognizing the need for changes in their organizations in response to cyber espionage and targeted attacks. Most countries in Europe, particularly NATO members and former Soviet satellite states, have reacted in a measured way. Their first step has been to set up a CERT (Computer Emergency Response Team) made up of members of the security, telecom, and military operations. These CERTs are to provide rapid communication in case of a cyber incident or even the outbreak of cyber hostilities. This is a reasonable first step.

The United States leads in its reaction to the perceived cyber threat, As noted in chapter 14, the Departments of Defense and Homeland Security have initiated many changes in their responses to cyber attacks. Studying what the United States does is valuable for other military organizations around the world.

These are just organizational changes. The changes coming to the executive branch will eventually see a cabinet-level position that is truly a cyber security czar. The person fulfilling this role will have direct access to the president and will drive cyber preparedness within the U.S. government. He will also provide guidance in the same way the head of the National Security Council provides actionable advice on affairs of state. While the Obama administration has vocalized its intent to create a cyber security coordinator, future administrations will need to institute a more powerful role to oversee all government cyber security measures and reactions to a rapidly changing cyber threatscape. Changes that the military and the other branches can expect to implement are similar to what the commercial sector has already applied. As cybercrime, insider malfeasance, and targeted attacks against data have risen, the investment in protective measures has followed suit. Governments are just beginning to understand this and are beginning to make commensurate investments.

Steps the United States will have to take (and other governments follow suit) to mitigate its cyber risk will include the following 10 points.

1. Establish responsibility for cyber security with real negative repercussions for those who fail to prevent breaches. This is no different from what businesses the world over have done in the past decade as they created roles such as Chief Information Security Officer (CISO), someone directly responsible for cyber security whose continued employment rides on how well an organization is protected. For civilians this means being fired; for the military this means court-martial, demotion, and expulsion for serious security breaches. The blame should not be pushed off on contractors. The only way that security is implemented is if someone's job is on the line. This goes all the way to the top, of course. The eventual role of cyber security czar will be responsible for enforcing responsibility all the way down the ranks. The cyber buck will stop with him or her.

2. Those responsible for locking down government networks and defending data need to be empowered with a set of strict rules. The United States already relies on the National Institute of Standards and Testing for such guidance. Future rules should include:

   i.   Access to all systems must be explicitly authorized.

   ii. All users must be identified and strongly authenticated. (Use of physical tokens or some other technology that strictly binds a user's credentials to his identity.)

   iii. All applications must be reviewed for security vulnerabilities and either fixed and put on a strict regimen of frequent security updates, or protected by application firewalls to prevent those vulnerabilities from being exploited.

   iv. All network attached systems must be scanned for vulnerabilities on a schedule. This is a large undertaking for an organization that has not systematized security, but until it is done the attackers will do it for you!

   v.   All network connections must be firewalled. As unbelievable as it may seem, there are many U.S. government servers and networks that still do not have even this rudimentary protection; or if they do the firewall rules do not explicitly deny all unwanted connections. Thus:

   vi. All firewalls must be configured to "deny all except that which is explicitly allowed."

   vii. All government networks must be mapped and understood. This is another large undertaking, but is no more than what most commercial networks have already done.

   viii. All data needs to be encrypted at rest.

   ix. All communication links need to be encrypted.

   x.   All intrusions need to be aggressively analyzed and appropriate responses executed. This entails the deployment of monitoring tools that can look into every packet and identify suspicious behavior.

3. Empower OMB (Office of Management and Budget, the government's accounting and auditing arm) to withhold funding to any agency that does not comply in a timely manner with measures 1 and 2.

4. Decentralize security management. One person cannot be effective in overseeing a cyber security policy. Security is everyone's responsibility, and the system should motivate responsible individuals to take action. (Policy is driven from the top down. Protection starts at the bottom.)

5. Fix the DHS information-sharing capability by learning from recent advances in social networking. Getting members of law enforcement, counterintelligence, or the military to collaborate effectively is not a task that can be accomplished by rolling out a quick-fix technology. In a secure environment individuals could find the most effective ways to communicate and share critical information.

6. Do not confuse security awareness campaigns with actual security improvements. The time, effort, and money that is spent on publicity campaigns could be better allocated to securing government networks.

7. While it seems to be the common reaction to a crisis, do not propose a new massive spending effort or any new departments to oversee cyber security. Security should be part of every computing infrastructure purchase and everyone's job. A centralized department for enforcing security will lead to infighting and bureaucracy as usual.

8. Make defense initiatives transparent. Do not cloak them in secrecy. Security by obscurity is impossible. Adversaries know what is being done. Congress, the press, and the people must know just what steps are being taken to protect the country's critical infrastructure.

9. Ensure that deploying long-needed security practices does not impair the free and open aspects of the Internet that have led to today's gains in communication and productivity. Spying on your citizens to discover terrorist plots can do more harm than good. The infrastructure needed to snoop on all communications (when it is not encrypted) could be too expensive for even the most profligate country.

10. Treat cyber offensive investments as secondary to defense. While there is a place for cyber espionage and customized attack methodologies, cyber defense should be the primary goal.

DETERRENCE

A recent published work from the National Research Center has explored the possibility of using the threat of cyber attack as a deterrent. The idea is that by threatening a massive preemptive or retaliatory cyber attack a nation could induce another country to concede or refrain from its own attacks. The product of intelligence operations has, historically, been a productive means of deterrence. Threatening an official with revelation of some secret activity could get him or his government to concede some point in diplomatic negotiations. But development of massive DDoS capability or mining critical undersea cables bears the risk of use that may cause more self-inflicted damage than benefit. One treatise on deterrence wrongly concludes that defense of networks is too expensive. But taking the steps listed here is not optional if an organization wants to continue to do business on the Internet. The attacks present today are enough to justify the investment in defense. It was only 10 years ago that most organizations would respond to warnings issued with every new major Microsoft vulnerability: "We can't take down thousands of servers every time Microsoft issues a patch!" Yet today most critical systems undergo a regular, systematic patching process. The rise of threats leads to the deployment of technologies to keep operations going. The earlier the need is recognized, the less likely that an expensive lesson will be learned from the inevitable successful attack.

INTERNATIONAL COOPERATION

In this early phase of the development of cyber warfare it is not surprising that international cooperation in countering the repercussions has not kept pace. Just as international treaties were created in response to the development of other weapons of war, expect cyber warfare to be treated in the same way. Today the definition of a "cyber act of war" is still in question. The consequences of engaging in cyber espionage and targeted attacks against nation-states have not been determined. Poison gas, land mines, and nuclear proliferation are all subjects of international conventions or treaties. As the use of cyber attacks rises look for the UN and other international bodies to meet and agree on these critical terms.

REPERCUSSIONS FOR BUSINESS

There are two aspects of cyberwar that are relevant to the nonmilitary enterprise. One is cyber espionage, the other is collateral damage from widespread cyber attacks. Banks, manufacturers, law firms, hospitals, schools, telecom companies, and local governments have become accustomed to the need for continuous investment in security tools and changing their policies to adapt to an ever-changing threat environment. Most of those investments have been to counter so-called random attacks: those that are spread throughout the Internet regardless of the target, like the ILOVEYOU virus or the SQL Slammer worm. They have also succumbed to direct attacks against their web servers, blog sites, or infrastructure that were motivated simply by their having a vulnerability that the attackers discovered. Running an unpatched version of

Microsoft Internet Information Server inevitably leads to an infection by the continuously circulating worms on the Internet. Or hackers exploit a vulnerability just because it exists—as Willie Sutton said when asked why he robbed banks: "because that's where the money is."

Cyberwar introduces a new class of attacker most enterprises have not geared up for: operatives of a nation-state or fanatic group. The stakes are higher for the attacker. The investment in technology, time, and effort for the attacker is higher and may even escalate to physical infiltration. In 2004 the London branch of Sumitomo Mitsui Bank suffered a near loss when bank robbers posed as cleaning staff and installed hardware devices on certain keyboards to record every keystroke. This allowed the attackers to attempt wire transfers with the credentials they captured. Motorola and Ford have both experienced data theft by Chinese nationals that downloaded key design data to CDs and attempted to transport them to competitors in China.

Enterprises must rethink their cyber defense strategies in light of the higher stakes incumbent in this new realm of cyber espionage. The major shift in thinking comes from a change in the trust granted to insiders.

An insider could be a contractor in India; a technician from a computer vendor; an employee in the front office, or, in the case of Société Générale Bank in France, a highly paid commodities trader. In that case a trader named Jérôme Kerviel used his knowledge of back-office operations to execute an end-run around controls that were supposed to prevent a trader from exposing the bank to too much risk. The result was a disastrous trading loss of $7 billion that could not have come at a worse time for the bank—January 2008, just when financial markets, already in turmoil, were least able to absorb a shock.

The primary change in business operations must be to start applying the same controls to trusted insiders that have been reserved for outsiders. It means deploying firewalls and Intrusion Prevention Systems internally as well as at outward-facing gateways. Every remote office must be firewalled from the home office. The data center and manufacturing shop floor must be segregated from the rest of the enterprise. Each school in a district must be firewalled so that students in one location cannot peer into other schools' data or networks. Applications must not be left open to all comers even if they have already obtained access to the internal network. Strong authentication in the form of physical tokens (digital ID cards) must be used to restrict access to only those explicitly allowed to use them. All access must be logged, and sophisticated monitoring tools should constantly be on the alert for behavior that violates the norm.

A first step to implementing controls at this level is to publish a policy statement and require every employee and privileged user to acknowledge reading it. But that is not near enough. Each policy must be enforced with effective technology that will block violations or at least alert when they are broken. This simultaneous publishing of a policy and enforcing it will prevent most insider abuse. The most effective way to deter illicit behavior is to instill the fear of being caught. If an end user knows he can access a health record, eavesdrop on an e-mail conversation, or use hacking tools to scan a network without being identified he is not deterred. Convincing him that every action on the internal network is monitored will prevent most such abuse.

Shawn Carpenter was responsible for monitoring network intrusions at Sandia. He used what was then state-of-the-art Intrusion Detection Systems (IDS) from Internet Security Systems, now a part of IBM. When he left Sandia he went to work for another government contractor, Mantech, which was working on a sophisticated tool that went far beyond the simple signature-matching capability of IDS. That product was spun out to high-tech investors, one of whom, Amit Yoran, was once the U.S. cyber security czar. Now Shawn spends his days helping large enterprises deploy and effectively tune these tools from Netwitness to discover and solve security incidents. Shawn is still at the forefront of cyber defense methodologies. The new generation of tools captures all network traffic and applies filters derived from many sources to identify when internal networks are communicating with known beaconing servers for botnets or attackers' IP addresses. This level of network monitoring, coupled with application-use monitoring down to the granular level of individual commands is required to change the security practices of an enterprise in order to counter the modern range of threats.

Along with this new mindset of reduced trust for insiders comes the need for a new level of support from business management and stakeholders. Most senior executives do not realize the extent to which their operations have become dependent on their IT infrastructure until disaster strikes and they discover that their data was exposed, their operations were vulnerable, and their financial results for the quarter have been negatively impacted. Major stockholders, boards of directors, and chief executives must all become familiar with the new risks they face and the new investments that must be made to shore up their defenses.

THE NEED FOR NEW THINKING

Unlike China and Russia, both of which maintain academies of military science, the United States has traditionally relied on nongovernment think tanks for guidance. This is good because it means that fresh thinking can be applied to new problems without the inherent bureaucracy of a government agency. In recent months several think tanks, including the Cato Institute, Hoover Institute, Heritage Foundation, and National Research Council have published documents on cyber warfare and defense. Most have not exhibited a technical understanding of the issues. This only speaks to the need for these think tanks to broaden their research capability by incorporating security technologists from industry in order to address this new realm of cyber warfare.

Wars are cathartic moments in history. They mark the end of countries and regimes and new beginnings for not just the assailants, but the world. Napoleon's wars of conquest and the two World Wars changed the makeup of Europe, but at the cost of millions of lives and the destruction of untold world wealth. Yet, along with conflict comes technological innovation and perhaps a readjustment of the balance of power that serves to create a more stable world.

What Are the Likely Repercussions of Cyberwar?
First the Bad:

The Internet and the human networks building around it are good. Human communication, it can be argued, is what defines us. Without speech, storytelling, writing, music, and performance art we are little more than herd animals scratching for a living. The Internet extends our reach individually. Through blogging, Twittering, and posting to Facebook we interact with more people on a daily basis than even a newspaper publisher or best-selling author of the previous century could.

A self-shot Numa Numa video of a young man mouthing the words to a pop song has been viewed over 6 million times. With 4,000 daily readers this author's blog is read by more people every day than read Thomas Paine's pamphlets. Cyberwar could impact the free expression of the good and the ugly. As nations take steps to secure their digital boundaries and root out evildoers, open access to the Internet is challenged. China, Germany, Myanmar, Australia, and the United States have all instituted restrictions on what can be said or done on the Internet. China monitors Internet communications and arrests and prosecutes those who are critical of the Communist Party and its actions, Germany has outlawed so-called hacking tools, Myanmar restricts access to websites, and Australia is building out the infrastructure for a national filtering capability that will protect its citizens from unsavory web content. The NSA spies on U.S. citizens in hopes of catching terrorist communication. These are reactions to perceived cyber threats, and as real cyber attacks continue their rise there will be more restrictions on communication and more fragmentation of what was a single global network into fiefdoms of content.

Military operations and intelligence-gathering agencies will create new capabilities to spy on each other, and even their own citizens, all in the name of improved defense and "homeland security."

Cyber attack capabilities will be created that could threaten the stability and availability of the Internet.

Legislation restricting the use of the Internet and regulating access will be enacted by well-meaning politicians. Social networks like Facebook and Twitter will change over time as more players use it for unintended purposes: to spy on individuals, gather news on the location of key personnel, and enlist participants in cyber conflict.

What Good Could Arise from Cyberwar?
Here Are Some Positive Developments

Governments that had weak cyber security will harden their systems in response to recognized threats and actual attacks. This is already happening around the world in response to both Chinese espionage activity and Russian-born DDoS attacks.

Businesses will also beef up their security, reducing the risk of exposure of key data to cyber spies and criminals alike.

Thanks to snooping by government entities, encryption technology will become more widely used. Vendors will create simpler forms of encryption and key management that are transparent to end users.

Individuals and companies will be able to conduct business on the Internet without fear of their communications being intercepted or tampered with.

Information technology practices and tools will advance to meet the challenge of encryption everywhere, DDoS attacks, vulnerability exploitation, and insider abuse. IT and communication infrastructures will become more resilient and reliable as a result.

Looking further out, it is possible to forecast that the increase in network security and data privacy technology will lead to better e-government; even the transition of democratic processes to the 'Net. New forms of financial instruments and ways of transmitting them securely will arise from a safer Internet.

The need for securing endpoints from spying eyes will give rise to better operating systems, and unbreakable device and application authentication that will protect intellectual property rights and enhance the viability of publishing models on the Internet.

While the repercussions of cyberwar will be disruptive and costly, there is hope that the benefits described here can take hold before, or even in spite of, the escalation into the kinetic conflict that will always be a looming possibility.

BIBLIOGRAPHY

Churchill, Winston S. *The Second World War: The Gathering Storm*. Cambridge: The Riverside Press, 1948.

CNN.com. "Homeland Security Seeks Cyber Counterattack System." October 4, 2008. www.cnn.com/2008/TECH/10/04/chertoff.cyber.security/.

Dulles, Allen W. *The Craft of Intelligence: America's Legendary Spy Master on the Fundamentals of Intelligence Gathering for a Free World*. Guilford, Conn.: Lyons Press, 2006. First published in 1963.

Goble, Paul. "Russia: Analysis from Washington—A Real Battle on the Virtual Front." *Radio Free Europe*. October 11, 1999. www.rferl.org/content/article/1092360.html.

Google News. "US Navy Creates Command to Maintain Cyber Supremacy." October 1, 2009. www.google.com/hostednews/afp/article/ALeqM5g05UQUihs3XAFGirrDnIsQtqdtw.

Gorman, Siobhan. "Computer Spies Breach Fighter-Jet Project." *Wall Street Journal*. April 21, 2009. online.wsj.com/article/SB124027491029837401.html.

Hyppönen, Mikko H. "Unrest in Ukraine." *F-Secure Weblog: News from the Lab*. October 31, 2007. www.f-secure.com/weblog/archives/00001305.html.

Intelligence.gov. "United States Intelligence Community—Who We Are." www.intelligence.gov/1-members.shtml.

Krebs, Brian. "Obama: Cyber Security Is a National Security Priority." *Washington Post*. May 29, 2009. voices.washingtonpost.com/securityfix/2009/05/obama_cybersecurity_is_a_natio.html.

Lawrence, T. E. *Seven Pillars of Wisdom: A Triumph*. New York: Anchor Books, 1991.

Libicki, Martin C. *Cyberdeterrence and Cyberwar*. Santa Monica, Calif.: RAND Corporation, 2009.

Lungu, Angela M. "War.com." *Joint Force Quarterly* (Spring/summer 2001). National Defense University Press. www.dtic.mil/doctrine/jel/jfq_pubs/0628 .pdf.

Marines.mil. "New Conceptual Paper Released." September 22, 2009. www .marines.mil/news/messages/Pages/MARADMIN0535-09.aspx.

Owens, William A., and Kenneth W. Dam. *Technology, Policy, Law, and Ethics Regarding U.S. Acquisition and Use of Cyberattack Capabilities*. Washington, D.C., 2009. Prepublication.

Paul, Ryan. "Pentagon E-mail Taken Down by Hackers." *Ars Technica*. June 22, 2007. arstechnica.com/security/news/2007/06/pentagon-e-mail-pwned-by -hackers.ars.

Radio Free Europe. "Newsline." May 3, 2007. www.rferl.org/content/article/ 1143864.html.

Reed, Thomas. *At the Abyss: An Insider's History of the Cold War*. New York: Presidio, 2005.

Sayer, Peter. "France Creates New National IT Security Agency." *CIO*. IDG News, July 10, 2009. www.cio.com.au/article/310622/france_creates_new _national_it_security_agency.

Schwartau, Winn. *Information Warfare Chaos on the Electronic Superhighway*. New York: Thunder's Mouth, distributed by Group West, 1994.

Shadowserver Foundation. August 13, 2008. www.shadowserver.org/wiki/ pmwiki.php/Calendar/20080813.

Thomas, Timothy L. *Decoding the Virtual Dragon*. Fort Leavenworth, Kans.: Foreign Military Studies Office, 2007.

U.S. Air Force. "24th Air Force Activated, 2 Units Realign in Joint Ceremony." www.af.mil/news/story.asp?id=123163831.

U.S. Army. *Our National Information Infrastructure: An Immediate Strategic Concern in National Security Policy*. By Brian P. Hamilton. U.S. Army War College, March 19, 2004. www.dtic.mil/cgi-bin/GetTRDoc?AD=ADA423907 &Location=U2&doc=GetTRDoc.pdf.

U.S. Congress. *Inadvertent File Sharing over Peer-to-Peer Networks*. Testimony July 24, 2007. www.gpo.gov/fdsys/pkg/CHRG-110hhrg11040150/pdf/CHRG-110 hhrg11040150.pdf.

U.S. Department of Homeland Security, USCERT. *Trusted Internet Connections (TIC) Initiative Statement of Capability Evaluation Report*. US-CERT/ISS LOB, June 4, 2008. georgewbush-whitehouse.archives.gov/omb/egov/documents/ 2008_TIC_SOC_EvaluationReport.pdf.

Verton, Dan. "Serbs Launch Cyberattack on NATO." *Federal Computer Weekly*, April 4, 1999. fcw.com/articles/1999/04/04/serbs-launch-cyberattack-on -nato.aspx.

Weiss, Gus W. "The Farewell Dossier—Duping the Soviets." *CIA.gov.* April 14, 2007. www.cia.gov/library/center-for-the-study-of-intelligence/csi -publications/csi-studies/studies/96unclass/farewell.htm.

Wu, Xu. *Chinese Cyber Nationalism: Evolution, Characteristics, and Implications.* Lanham, Md.: Lexington Books, 2007.

NOTES

CHAPTER 2

1. Captain Powers was captured and imprisoned by the Soviets for almost two years and eventually exchanged in a swap for the KGB operative Colonel Vilyam Fisher in a cinematic scene at Berlin's Glienicke Bridge. He died piloting a traffic helicopter for KNBC in Los Angeles in 1968.

2. Xu Wu, *Chinese Cyber Nationalism: Evolution, Characteristics, and Implications* (Lanham, Md.: Lexington Books, 2007).

3. Allen W. Dulles, *The Craft of Intelligence* (Guilford, Conn.: The Lyons Press, 2006). First published in 1963.

4. See Timothy L. Thomas, *Decoding the Virtual Dragon* (Fort Leavenworth, Kans.: Foreign Military Studies Office, 2007), 333.

5. Cited in Thomas, *Virtual Dragon*, 66.

CHAPTER 4

1. Richard Norton-Taylor, "Titan Rain: How Chinese Hackers Targeted Whitehall," *Guardian*, September 5, 2007, www.guardian.co.uk/technology/2007/sep/04/news.internet.

2. "Espionage Report: Merkel's China Visit Marred by Hacking Allegations," *Spiegel Online*, August 27, 2007, www.spiegel.de/international/world/0,1518,502169,00.html.

3. John Goetz and Marcel Rosenbach, "Cyber Spies: 'Ghostnet' and the New World of Espionage," *Spiegel Online*, April 10, 2009, www.spiegel.de/international/world/0,1518,618478,00.html.

4. *Space War*, "French government falls prey to cyber-attacks 'involving China,'" September 8, 2007, www.spacewar.com/reports/French_government _falls_prey_to_cyber-attacks_involving_China_999.html.

5. Philip Dorling, "Cyber Attack on Diplomats," *Canberra Times*, August 17, 2009, www.canberratimes.com.au/news/national/national/general/cyber -attack-on-diplomats/1597327.aspx.

6. Demetri Sevastopulo, "Chinese Hack into White House Network," *Financial Times*, November 6, 2008, www.ft.com/cms/s/0/2931c542-ac35-11dd-bf71-000077b07658.html?nclick_check=1.

7. *Newsweek*, "Hackers and Spending Sprees," November 5, 2008, www .newsweek.com/id/167581.

CHAPTER 5

1. Siobhan Gorman, "Computer Spies Breach Fighter-Jet Project," *Wall Street Journal*, April 21, 2009, online.wsj.com/article/SB124027491029837401 .html.

CHAPTER 6

1. Erich Follath and Holger Stark, "The Story of 'Operation Orchard': How Israel Destroyed Syria's Al Kibar Nuclear Reactor," *Spiegel Online*, November 2, 2009, www.spiegel.de/international/world/0,1518,658663-2,00.html.

2. David A. Fulghum, Robert Wall, and Amy Butler, "Israel Shows Electronic Prowess," *Aviation Week*, November 25, 2007, www.aviationweek.com/aw/ generic/story.jsp?id=news/aw112607p2.xml&headline=Israel%20Shows%20El ectronic%20Prowess&channel=defense.

3. Nart Villanueve, "Defacement Flare-Up & Truce," December 1, 2008, www.nartv.org/2008/12/01/defacement-flare-up-truce/.

CHAPTER 8

1. *Wikipedia*, "Crowdsourcing," en.wikipedia.org/wiki/Crowdsourcing.

2. Cited in "Chinese Hacktivists Waging People's Information Warfare against CNN," *Dancho Danchev's Blog—Mind Streams of Information Security Knowledge*, ddanchev.blogspot.com/2008/04/chinese-hacktivists-waging -peoples.html.

CHAPTER 9

1. Radio Free Europe, "Newsline," May 3, 2007, www.rferl.org/content/article/1143864.html.

CHAPTER 10

1. Angela M. Lungu, "War.com," *Joint Force Quarterly* 2001, Spring/summer, National Defense University Press. www.dtic.mil/doctrine/jel/jfq_pubs/0628.pdf.

2. Paul Goble, "Russia: Analysis from Washington—A Real Battle on the Virtual Front," Radio Free Europe/Radio Liberty, October 11, 1999, www.rferl.org/content/article/1092360.html.

3. See F-Secure, www.f-secure.com/weblog/archives/00001305.html; and www.axisglobe.com/article.asp?article=1419 oct-10-2007.

CHAPTER 13

1. Cited in Timothy L. Thomas, *Decoding the Virtual Dragon* (Fort Leavenworth, Kans.: Foreign Military Studies Office, 2007), 75.

2. Thomas C. Reed, *At the Abyss: An Insider's History of the Cold War* (New York: Presidio, 2004), 268.

CHAPTER 14

1. Brian Krebs, "Obama: Cyber Security Is a National Security Priority," Security Fix, *Washington Post*, May 29, 2009, voices.washingtonpost.com/securityfix/2009/05/obama_cybersecurity_is_a_natio.html.

2. U.S. Department of Homeland Security, "Trusted Internet Connections Initiative: Statement of Capability Evaluation Report," June 4, 2008, georgewbush-whitehouse.archives.gov/omb/egov/documents/2008_TIC_SOC_EvaluationReport.pdf.

3. www.cnn.com/2008/TECH/10/04/chertoff.cyber.security/.

4. U.S. Air Force, "24th Air Force Activated, 2 Units Realign in Joint Ceremony," August 18, 2009, www.af.mil/news/story.asp?id=123163831.

5. AFP, "US Navy Creates Command to Maintain Cyber Supremacy," October 1, 2009, www.google.com/hostednews/afp/article/ALeqM5g05UQUihs3XAFGirrDnIsQtqdtw.

6. U.S. Marine Corps, "New Conceptual Paper Released," September 2, 2009, www.marines.mil/news/messages/Pages/MARADMIN0535-09.aspx.

7. Peter Sayer, "France Creates New National IT Security Agency," *CIO*, July 10, 2009, www.cio.com.au/article/310622/france_creates_new_national_it _security_agency.

INDEX

ABOUT THE AUTHOR

Richard Stiennon, security expert and analyst, is known for shaking up the industry and providing actionable guidance to vendors and end users. He is the founder of IT-Harvest, an independent analyst firm that researches the 1,200 IT security vendors, and the author of the security blog ThreatChaos.com. He has been the chief marketing officer for Fortinet, Inc., a leading UTM vendor, and the vice president of Threat Research at Webroot Software, where he followed and wrote about the rising tide of spyware. He was also the vice president of Research at Gartner, Inc., where he covered security topics including firewalls, intrusion detection, intrusion prevention, security consulting, and managed security services for the security and privacy group. He is a holder of Gartner's Thought Leadership Award and was named "One of the 50 most powerful people in Networking" by Network World.

Mr. Stiennon has had speaking engagements in 28 countries on six continents. He has written for *Network World* (IDG) and *CIOUpdate* (Jupiter Media). His blog is syndicated at InfosecIsland.com and Forbes.com